THE GOLDEN SUN

THE
GOLDEN SUN

ROBERT SHAFER

NEW DEGREE PRESS

COPYRIGHT © 2021 ROBERT SHAFER

All rights reserved.

THE GOLDEN SUN

ISBN   978-1-63676-825-0   *Paperback*
          978-1-63730-217-0   *Kindle Ebook*
          978-1-63730-269-9   *Ebook*

ACKNOWLEDGMENTS

Thank you so much to all the people who have helped me on this journey to publish! One never really knows just how much goes into the book publishing process, and I'm so grateful for all the support. It would not have been possible if not for the many people who lent their aid. Thank you all for helping make this book a reality.

To my beta readers, thank you for reading parts of the manuscript before publication and giving me your feedback.

Shannon Stromberg, Kevin Song, Nathan Sander, Winona Wang, and Damian Yazzi.

To my editors, teachers, and the many others who work behind the scenes at New Degree Press, thank you for the ample advice and direction you gave in developing and revising the story.

Jacqueline Claire Reiniri Calamia, Mozelle Jordan, Kristin Noland, Leah Pickett, Haley Newlin, Brian Bies, and Eric Koester.

To those who have supported me by preordering, sharing, donating, or simply giving advice, thank you so much.

Shannon Stromberg, Darren and Lisa Shafer, Junko Adams, Joyce Shafer, David Mendes and Vibhati Kulkarny, Catherine Forman, Kara Martinez, Richard and Mary-Ann Shafer, Gregory Massoud, Max Gruner and Amy Loyd, Julia Shafer and Mihir Shah, Denise Fligner, Frank and Chuc Oberlinger, Shaun Gehres, Cherrie Boyer, Aerlin Decker, Alexandra Ravano, Simon Staskewitsch, Scott Forman, Justin and Juniper Decker, Renee and Jeff Kinney, Jenny Culver, Kate Nelson, Lenin Diaz and Craig Smith, Tommy Roe, Skylar Forman, Mike Hsu, Jason DeBonis and Leslie Jackson, Raye Myers, Michele Chwastiak, Cathy Drake, Jacob Buehler and Amber Heyes, Sowang Kundeling, Joe Coventry, Natasha Kolb, Maxine Lui, Annie and Hayes Shimp, Karen Lyall, Jill Slominski, Toru Nyunoya, Dorothy Melloy, Eric Koester, Nathan Flores, Connor Bugni, Yuika and Tatsuya Norii, Cesar Baca, Kevin Song, Cecilia Gao, Marisa Garcia, Alejandra Campillo, Augustino Escandon, Cameron Rogers, Timi Adeniyi, Erin Pickett, Riley Weinstein, Charles Fan, Andrew Wolz, Sophie Kim, Nathan Sander, Alex McLaughlin, Ardra Shephard, Kylan Butler, Brynne Anderson, Julia Walsdorf, Andrew Jogi, Celeste Rudolfo, Jemima Lewis, Abraham Yohannes, Estevan Hutchinson, Ruby Carlson, Jadyn Gardner, Erin Mantsch, Sienna Hsu, Andrew Pick-Roth, Samuèle Baca, Kevin Zhang, Claudia Farrelly, Esther Marcos, Julia Ross, John Kelley, Dominic Martin, Sophia Jaramillo, Angela Ornelas, Francesca Abruzzo, Emily Brodie, Harvey Vaughan, Nicholas Miliatis, Rebecca Torrez, Erin McBurney, Erin Goff, Kevin Xue, Jessica Gallardo, Arlie Bledsoe, Gavin Hearne, Timber Underhill, Lucas Frey, Maya Bhanot, Ashanti Prosper, Göktuğ Bender, Greg Medina-Kenyon, Njaka Rasamoelina, and Luis Jamora.

CONTENTS

*To my wonderful father and mother,
whom I thank for everything.*

*"Don't worry, we shall have wonderful dreams,
and when we wake up, it'll be spring."*

—TOVE JANSSON, *FINN FAMILY MOOMINTROLL*

*"All the lives we don't experience
are merely myths to us."*

—BENYAMIN, *GOAT DAYS*

NOTE FROM THE AUTHOR

Dear Readers,

There are many things I had set out to do when writing *The Golden Sun*, but I think my most principal aim was to simply reflect on myself and my world. I started writing this book as a way to contemplate and respond to current events and cultural trends, whose significance has been gleaned from various conversations with people over the years, my education thus far, and from news and social media. Accordingly, there are many characters in this book, each with a different way of looking at the world, a different set of values, and different motivations. They're all flawed and filled, hopefully, with a healthy dose of moral ambiguity.

The majority of *The Golden Sun* takes place on a train—following the journey of a rootless protagonist who is traveling to his mother's hometown, drawing from her past in order to ground himself in his present life. In this same way, I try to take you on a "journey of observation" by presenting an assortment of characters, from an old woman taking one last trip while still spry enough, to a wanna-be revolutionary on his way to start a political movement, to a dissatisfied artist trying to reconnect with her past. I hope the choices and values of these characters make you deeply consider your own values, your own sense of morality, and your own conception of self. We all fall into the habit of thinking we know ourselves and our values, but when we reflect on it more, we often find that there's still a lot more to discover.

I also found as I was writing that I was putting a lot of my own ideas and sentiments into the characters and mood of the book. Indeed, all the characters come from some part of myself—even if they themselves do and believe in things that I personally don't. But in thinking more on what this book is about, I started to realize my ideas and sentiments aren't all that unique. In many ways, I found this book reflects how many people in our internet era view the world. Of course, I can't claim that everyone feels the way I do, but I think you will find that, on a deeper, baser level, the feelings conveyed in this book are shared by many in our times.

Part of the reason I think it's good to write about this now is that my generation, the loosely defined *Generation Z*, is at a precipice. We are no longer at home or in high school but beginning to go out into the world—to college and to the workforce. In other words, we are the up-and-coming generation, starting to be the real *movers and shakers* of the world.

We are also the first generation to have grown up inundated with the internet and social media. This is an important point because the role of modern technology and media in our times is not well-understood. Specifically, the popularization of the internet and social media have presented us with a paradigm shift, the consequences of which are still poorly understood and almost criminally neglected by the layperson. Media, social or journalistic, is often viewed simply as a tool—a way to keep *in the know* and stay in touch with friends and family, but it is far more than that. It is not simply a tool but rather a perspective—a medium—in itself. Because of that, it carries much ontological baggage that we cannot afford to ignore. Our lives are not simply documented on the internet—they are lived out through it.

In addition, with the role of the community increasingly being forgotten in our times, almost by default, this vacuum of belonging and meaning is being replaced largely by social media. In other words, our generation's alienation is only further compounded by our maladroit attempts to connect with others through meaningless and insidious but entertaining activities. As one more curmudgeonly character says toward the end of *The Golden Sun*, our current world is a "tundra of stunted lives and half-cultivated meaning." While it is a rather dramatic statement, it nonetheless holds a great deal of truth. I have intentionally set this book to be in the early twentieth century technologically so that it is possible to reflect on these changes modern media bring us, without being too distracted by the flash and bang of modern technology itself. I do this so as to emphasize the importance of the actual human experience. To understand the nature of the debasement and alienation of our times, we must understand the nature of media and technology.

For these reasons, I imagine the most generalized characteristics of our generation and the subsequent ones will be cynicism, pragmatism, alienation, and powerlessness. I say this knowing that this book has been written entirely during the COVID-19 pandemic, and my perception has largely been cultivated during the period of teen angst that it seems all generations have. Regardless, it's because of this perception that there's a certain cynicism and world-weariness in this book.

At the same time, I didn't want to dwell on these feelings in a dreary or self-important way, but rather I included them in order to ask the questions, "What do we do with these feelings of meaninglessness, and where do we go from here?" In this way, I am asking questions that are not unique to my generation, but rather I think, to the world at large. However, I cannot say I'm honestly trying to provide answers in this book (though many of the characters do try to do this for themselves); but rather, I try to ask and describe. I wrote this book in an attempt to hold up a mirror to society and to the reader. In the broadest sense, I wrote this book for anyone who doesn't feel satisfied with their life; for anyone who ever asks themselves, "Is this all there is?" Thus, it's up to the reader to develop their own solution, if there is one.

This is a rather personal book filled with rather personal thoughts and opinions. I feel, however, I do have something of value to say. Perhaps it will come off as naïve ramblings, and perhaps you'll get something from it. I imagine most likely it'll be a mix of the two. But in any case, for whatever this book comes to mean for you, I hope you like it. Thank you for reading.

1

It was a muggy morning that Cezal awoke to find his dog dead in the kitchen. She was old, and so it didn't come as much of a surprise. Her body was gray, lying like an uncomfortable lump in an odd spot on the faded brown, tiled floor. The house was quiet enough after his mother's death a few years ago, but now, with the dog gone, it was a truly deafening silence. He stood for some time in the doorway of his bedroom, looking at it, unsure of how to feel.

The house was sturdy and didn't overheat easily, but in the summer, the heat gets everywhere—there is no real escape. The best Cezal could do in such times was keep the windows open throughout the day and draw the drapes. He watered the geraniums in their flower boxes that hung from the windows and prepared to take the dog to the countryside to be buried. She was not too big, though nor could she fit into his suitcase very easily.

He ended up carrying her in a burlap sack, hoisted over his back. As he walked down the cobbled street, the neighbors looked at him strangely, though it's no wonder why. The damp sound of old, worn shoes replaced the standard clack of his dress shoes. His gait sounded burdened by something heavy. They could tell it was Cezal's dog in the sack because after leaving the door slightly ajar or peeking out of their window, instead of avoiding his glance in their direction as they usually did when they knew they were caught being nosy, most locked eyes with him and made some gesture of sympathy or understanding.

The following days, he spent in reflection. *Perhaps it's time I move on.* He and the dog had been good companions for one another. "She keeps you young," his mother had often remarked. They went and enjoyed the reawakening of nature together in the spring, endured the heat in the summer, foraged together in the fall, and enjoyed warm soup in the winter. His neighbors, in fact, had often accused him of spoiling her when they learned how frequently his hearty soups, often with plenty of vegetables and good quality meat, were not simply for Cezal and his mother, but rather for *all* members of the household.

The afternoon sun stained the rolling hills red with intensity. The hole took longer to dig than Cezal had thought, and he had trouble motivating himself to fill it back in after placing her body there. *What do I have here? What is my legacy? No one misses a banker.* His white shirt was covered in sweat, and he found himself constantly wiping his brow. Despite his efforts to keep clean, he found his face feeling as though caked with dust.

He sat on the hill to rest and looked toward the city, its striking buildings scarring the landscape with stone, wood, and paint. Afternoons are always nice there. The buildings are close enough together that there is some respite from the intensity of the sun, painting the outer walls and ground a particular red—a wonderful crimson. Kids often play outside at that time, and so one comes to associate that color with the sounds of laughter and yelling bouncing between walls.

* * *

Cezal's mother was from Sectohal, a very large, sparsely populated region far in the East. He'd long forgotten which town, in particular, she grew up in, his mother having been the kind that preferred the sound of silence to what she used to term "banal noise." She was, of course, of a stricter, more somber time. Yes, she was rather closed off, some would say. This was her upbringing—very conservative by all estimations. One didn't talk of politics or religion, or even of hopes and dreams, except to a very select few. Cezal found himself in the former category and so was ostensibly a stranger to her history and interior life.

* * *

For the next week, he got his affairs more or less in order; asked his neighbor, Miss Elmyta, to look over his house—rent it out, furniture and all. He asked her to give him monthly updates by telegram and send him half the profit from the rent, quarterly. The other half was hers, as the landlord, to keep.

A cheekier person may already wonder if Cezal fully realized the purposelessness of his life. It can be assured, though, he was well aware of this fact—he simply didn't care, at least not that much. There were times when it had bothered him, certainly, but after a while of living in such unsatisfactory conditions, one must ask oneself, "Am I going to actually make any changes in my life?" Cezal had asked this very question, and his answer to that, while his mother and dog were alive, was simply *no*. And so, for that portion of his life, he did his best to simply put it out of mind. The same people who are wondering if he realized his own futility are probably also guessing he's the kind of person who would easily become a *victim of fate*. To that, however, a halfhearted no could be said. His mother, though, ever the unaware one, was such a victim—Cezal himself even admitted to that, if perhaps in a more loving way. Regardless, he saw her unhappiness and did his best to extricate himself from such a fate. Largely, one may suppose, it had worked.

* * *

The day he went to buy the train ticket was the first day the heat hadn't been unbearable. There was a pleasant breeze and even the lingering humidity from the prior day's late afternoon rain. It was nice for him to see people about, enjoying the parks, the children walking with their parents or whomever, eating their ice cream with single-minded enjoyment. The tickets he bought were the cheapest available. Why did he buy such cheap ones? There were multiple reasons: He deemed it unnecessary to buy nicer ones—he was in no rush to get to Sectohal, and, from the more romantic part of himself, he couldn't help but hear the mantra, "It's about the journey, not the destination," echoing about. In either case, he usually found those who traveled first class to be rather incapable of interesting conversation.

This said, after Cezal bought his tickets, for the first leg of the journey, he saw the first-class train would be connected to his. Only after they passed the second major city would the train split and those in the 'Emerald Class' get priority passage, or rather, those in the third class lose their priority passage. Indeed, if one were to have compared travel times, even standard mail would have arrived in Briedavga, the capital of Sectohal, more quickly. It was to be an uncomfortable journey, of course, but that was an inconvenience Cezal underestimated and thus didn't care too horribly about. Nothing, he thought, that a bit of patience wouldn't ameliorate.

* * *

On the day of Cezal's departure, he brought with him one suitcase and one rather small canvas bag. He wore canvas pants and a blue linen shirt with brown leather shoes and a straw hat. It was late summer, and by then, the dog days were coming to an end, and the world was beginning to awaken once more. The train itself was maroon on the exterior and fitted with personal cabins aptly named after their capacity; that is, a single, a double, or a quadruple. Cezal had the double, and when he stepped on the train, he noted the scratched lacquer on the wooden panels and the dingy carpet with a rather repulsive pattern. He went to his predesignated cabin and slid the door open—there were two beds on opposite sides of the cabin with a small table equipped with a lamp that was between them. Given the cramped quarters, it seemed that the bed would also have to function as the chair for the table. Each bed had white sheets and a small storage space above them. Lastly, between the two beds and above the table was a window. Sitting on the bed opposite of his was an old woman with a slouched back who introduced herself as Iljantva. She was to be his cabinmate for the following days.

He settled in, and soon, the desert began to flow past them with its shrubbery and vistas, glowing red and purple in the afternoon light. Birds flew overhead and into the distance, passing out of view due to the changing angle of the train. The train itself, of course, had its ever-present click and clack to it, decorating the time and giving rhythm to the relative silence. Iljantva looked out the window too, and they stayed that way for a while. She began to read a book. Sometime later, he got up to get tea and asked her if she would like some.

She looked at him and smiled. "Oh yes, that would be quite nice. Thank you."

Over the following days, the landscape transformed from a desert to an increasingly alpine environment—the kind Sectohal was known for, though they were still quite some ways away. During this time, Cezal and Iljantva got to talking more. They enjoyed the pleasantries of conversation that two strangers who meet while traveling get to indulge in. She was a florist and journalist back in her hometown—a combination of professions that earned her a certain regard among the townspeople. The village she was going to was known for its fields of flowers and flower festivals in the spring. Similar to Cezal, she wasn't sure if it was to be an extended vacation or a long-term living arrangement.

He came to see her propensity for having what she termed "conversations on matters of the heart."

"I don't have much time to waste," she once explained, "so you'll have to forgive me if I tend to skip over chit-chat and talk on personal topics early on."

The pine trees sauntered past the window of the train car, just as they had yesterday, and the day before, and the day before that. The sun was milder at this latitude and was, at this time of the day, nearing the horizon. The train car made the dull, rhythmic clack that paced time while en route. Cezal leaned back in a half-daze, having just woken up from a nap and enjoying the scene before him. Nightfall would soon come. He looked to the bed opposite to him and saw Iljantva wasn't there. She often went to the dining car rather early.

She returned sometime later with two cups of tea in tow. "Both cups are actually for me," she joked when Cezal instinctually reached for the one she had gotten for him. He paused for a second as they locked eyes and then laughed. They sat in silence for some time, sipping absentmindedly from the glass teacups. The trees flowed past, glimmering in the afternoon light.

"I hope you don't mind my asking," Cezal said, "why is it that you're moving now? Why not stay where you've been for so long?"

She smiled a bit as she turned to look at Cezal and shrugged her shoulders, her milky eyes alternating between Cezal and the window. "I think, really, for many of the same reasons as you. I'm not getting younger, and there's much of the world I've yet to explore. Even though it's just a little corner more that I will come to know, at least I will get that, and that's something quite nice in its own right." She smiled a bit and tilted her head as she spoke. Cezal nodded his head, and they sat in silence for a few moments more.

"What I've come to learn," Iljantva broke in again, "is that, in general, people live with the sense of urgency of an immortal. Take it from me: There does come a time when it really *is* too late for some things—a time after which 'to start over' simply isn't a meaningful phrase." She turned to look out of the window again. "I think, especially now, finitude is something relatively forgotten. It's something I certainly forgot for quite some time." She paused. Cezal didn't know how to respond, so he did little more than grunt as elegantly as he could.

"But you know," Iljantva finally continued, "it's nice to be reminded of things you once forgot. In a way, I suppose, it's nice that we forget some things. Because then there can be those who remind us, and we get to rediscover something once again."

Cezal smiled a bit. "I guess that's true, but certainly some things shouldn't be forgotten, wouldn't you say?"

She looked back at him and chuckled. "Of course so!" And she threw her head up to laugh. "But it's bound to happen. It always comes to be that people forget the important things and have to be reminded once again. One can only hope they take what they are reminded of to heart before it's too late. And in my experience, most people are hopeless romantics, but as that is, many are so bound by their ego, they romanticize themselves: their problems, their struggles, their self-conception, their identity—they think it makes them who they *are*," she scoffed gently. "But it's far harder to be a happier person, a better person, a whatever person, if you're in love with the way you are or feel at the moment. People put their identity into the most foolish things, I must say, and I don't exclude myself from this. Still, most often, it's detrimental to one's growth and development. They secretly take pride in things they shouldn't because it's more comforting for the time being. It's hard to let go of the perception you have of yourself, but it's necessary if you want to keep moving forward. Define yourself by the ultimate goal—your ultimate end. Really, deep down, people just want to love and be loved. Cherished and feel cherished. Need and be needed." She turned to look directly at Cezal. "Most likely, deep down, that's all you really want too." She gave a kind smile. "And if that's so, then orient yourself to those goals. How do you get there?"

She paused a moment.

"I hope I haven't seemed too direct in interpreting your life and what you may need to hear. Based on our conversations these last few days, you do sound somewhat lost, and as they say, advice is cheap, so I figured there's no harm in giving my two cents."

Cezal assured her that her advice was welcome, and spent the following hours looking at the passing trees.

* * *

Another night, Iljantva was out. Where? Cezal didn't know. She had simply told him earlier, "not to wait up." In his comfortability though, he made the mistake of keeping his cabin door open, which was, as Cezal came to learn, the sign on the train that anyone was free to come in to socialize. Of course, at that time of night, a demure crowd was not something worth expecting. A drunken man who introduced himself as Bekochan wandered in and sat down on Iljantva's bed, leaning against the wall by the window.

Cezal quickly moved to get Iljantva's stuff away from Bekochan, to his own side of the cabin and asked the stranger what he was doing there.

"Oh, sorry, I hope I'm not imposing," he trailed off, looking more in Cezal's general direction than at Cezal himself. "You seem like a nice bloke, eh? You want something to drink?"

Cezal declined and moved his bag closer to him.

Bekochan half hiccupped, and half burped into his plaid shirt, then, out of his glass teacup, took a sip of what could be reasonably assumed to be straight vodka and, in a single, surprisingly elegant motion, put the cup down on the table and leaned across, toward Cezal, as though about to reveal a secret. His breath, of course, stank, and Cezal could confirm that it was indeed vodka—the cheap kind that smelled faintly of stale cheese.

"I was born with a special gift, you know," Bekochan said, his lips fumbling into the position of a wry smile as he tried to look mysterious, raising his eyebrow.

"Is that so?" Cezal asked, still on guard.

"Yes, though I have told few about it…" he trailed off and scanned the cabin as though suspicious. "Seeing as to how we're alone, I think it is safe for me to tell you." He took long pauses between each breath, and Cezal, seeing the sluggishness with which he moved, took to noting the rhythmic clack of the train tracks, counting the number of cycles it would go through before Bekochan began to talk again. Two clacks, four clacks, even seven clacks at one point when he stopped talking midsentence. Docile indeed, like he just wanted someone to talk to.

"You see," Bekochan began again, "I know nothing is real—not you, not this train, not any of this." He intentionally waved his arm around to the other two seats in the cabin and outside the window, to the darkness. "What is loneliness, my friend, when we can never not be alone? And by that logic, when you are with your friends and family, when you are gathered around a great fire, and all is well and merry, and everyone is singing and feeling understood, you are just as alone as you are now—with none of them around. And yet—"

It was at this point when there was a sincere twinkle in his eye as he tilted his head slightly toward Cezal and raised his arm a bit, pointing with his finger half at him, and half at nothing in particular. "I didn't feel alone *then*. So, my friend, one must ask, why should I feel more alone now? Don't let the world trick you! Because it's all one great trick. I am simply the spectator of a poorly written drama." He hiccupped again and leaned back, letting out a sigh as he stared out the window.

Soon later, he fell asleep, slumped over in a seemingly uncomfortable position and after not too much longer, Cezal woke him up and shooed him out so that Iljantva wouldn't have to deal with him when she returned.

2

———

The farmhouse was sturdy—made of limestone bricks and a roof of reddened clay tile. The lavender fields that the house served extended all the way to the horizon; that is, from the perspective of the twelve-year-old Iljantva, whose specially made shoes made it so she could touch the tops of the lavender when on her tippy toes, but nonetheless still couldn't see the entire estate. Once spring set in, it was her job to wake up before the sun and make coffee for her aunt, which she always left on the stove before going out to harvest the lavender. The best time to cut, according to her aunt, was just after the morning dew evaporated from the flowers, but before the sun came to be too hot. So Iljantva had to work quickly during this season, getting some twenty to twenty-five bundles every morning, which she dutifully strung and hung upside down on the line near the house.

Iljantva's mother used to always have her wear a wide-brimmed, straw hat with a thick, crimson bow tied around it whenever she would go outside in the spring and summer, even if the sun were obscured or it were early morning. Once Iljantva came to live with her aunt, she made it oft clear she needn't wear the hat when the sun wasn't out, but Iljantva always insisted. And so, when her aunt called her in to eat her eggs, she would always look in what direction to yell by finding where, among the sea of lavender, the crimson hat was bobbing.

"Janka!" the aunt called. "Come inside, yes? Breakfast is ready."

No longer did Iljantva run to get from place to place, nor did her smile have that particular gleam unique to young children. *Is it good to grow up?* The aunt often wondered this when observing the nearly adolescent Iljantva. Of course, she had only lived with her aunt for about four years, so perhaps much of the groundwork for growing up had, by many estimations, already been lain.

But she felt old. And how old will she be once Janka is her own age? Dead, perhaps, though she supposed, one needn't be so morbid.

Iljantva didn't eat her eggs with as much vigor anymore either.

"Would you like some juice, Janka?"

"No, thank you."

"Okay," she replied, sipping her coffee.

How nice it was to feel needed.

* * *

Cezal was sitting on his own one evening in the dinner car, a particularly cramped part of the train with small two-to-four-person booths with maroon upholstery and subpar lighting. At the far end, where Cezal sat, there was the canteen that, at this time, served only hot, mushroom soup, burnt coffee, and rye bread. He was enjoying his after-dinner coffee, thinking of nothing in particular, when a vaguely stubby man with rosy cheeks, who appeared to be in his early thirties, got up from his own table somewhat farther away from the kitchen side of the car and approached Cezal, glass in hand.

"Hello!" he called.

Cezal turned to face the man. "Yes," the latter exclaimed. "You'll have to forgive me for being so forward… eah… well, why should I feel embarrassed? You wouldn't happen to have studied in Bjumme?"

Cezal gave him a politely puzzled expression to cover his bemusement.

"You're the famous sculptor, are you not?" he asked, squeezing into the booth to sit across from Cezal.

"No," Cezal chuckled somewhat apprehensively, "I'm afraid I'm not."

The stubby man balked. "Why have you laughed at what I said? Does it sound absurd?" He paused a bit to take a sip of his drink, a sort of faux scorn adorning his face. "You know," he began again, "those who laugh at that which seems ridiculous are those who put up imaginary walls around which they structure their lives. They have rules they themselves likely don't perceive, but they nonetheless confine themselves by."

The man began to unfurl the napkin in his place setting and started fidgeting with it before continuing. "Humor is a form of bonding. It is a way of feeling the other person out and understanding how they make sense of the world. To discover one has a similar life story or a similar taste in music is another type of humor—another type of bonding to be had. It's simply another form of social coercion." He suddenly looked up, thinking himself dramatic, "So humor me this, *mon frère*, why do you laugh?"

Who is this asshole? Cezal wondered, though of course, he was rather the kind to suffer fools and indulge in the vices of regrettable companions. And at least this joker gave quasi-insightful advice.

So Cezal lifted his glass to meet his new companion's slightly shaky one and took a deep breath. "I honestly don't know," he began, "but it sounds like a rather profound question, so, cheers to that, *mon frère.*"

Cezal assumed the subdued facetiousness of his remark would be lost on the man. And indeed, he was right. A mischievous smile spread over his face as he raised his glass. "Oh, I like you. Cheers."

They both took a sip—he, his drink, and Cezal, his coffee.

The other patrons were sparsely talking. The families had long since left, so it was mostly single people enjoying a cup of tea or coffee, reading their paper in a public place, or simply people watching.

"So tell me… eh, what's your name?" Cezal asked once their cups were both placed on the table.

The man waved his hands dramatically in the air. "Oh, how rude of me! I'm Dzhes Ievlagenabad. And what's your name?"

"I'm Ce—"

Dzhes quickly raised his index finger. "No, no, don't tell me," he quickly added. "I mistook you for Ebem Nuzhdlabet— you know, the famous sculptor. He and I were flatmates in Bjumme. Anyhow, I'd prefer not to know your real name. Rather, I'll call you Ebem."

Cezal stared at him blankly as the car rocked gently back and forth.

"Surely that doesn't bother you, does it?" Dzhes asked innocently. "Do go on."

Cezal went on, "Yes… so, em, Dzhes, where are you headed?"

"Ah, well, yes, I'm here on a business trip of sorts. You see, I'm heading east to meet a potential client for our company. Mergers and acquisitions; that sort of thing. But that's all rather boring. What are you drinking?" He looked into Cezal's coffee cup. "Coffee! No, that won't do. I'll tell you what, Ebem, for old times sake, why don't you join us in the cocktail car, on the other side of the kitchen."

"You go through the kitchen?"

Dzhes smiled with a glint. "Yes, it's quite something, isn't it? We all think it's a riot!"

Cezal, of course, was inclined to refuse but, in the spirit of his voyage, agreed to go.

"Oh wonderful!" replied Dzhes, his cherry face lighting up. "I have to relieve myself, but I'll see you in the back car—just head right through the kitchen and if anyone asks, just tell them I invited you."

He stumbled away, and Cezal finished his coffee, took a deep breath, and stared out the window for a few minutes. There is a certain lingering warmth to the night in summer, and the trees are reflective of that.

Cezal finished steeping in the moment, took another deep breath, and stood up. He headed through the kitchen to the back dining car filled, undoubtedly, with enough tawdry people to satisfy the hunger of even the most shameless sycophant.

The back car did not disappoint and was filled with as much low-budget grandeur as one could accommodate in a single train car. Instead of normal dining booths, there were instead only cocktail tables with some leather, overstuffed chairs near the caboose window. The lights had a different, softer hue and mingled well with the velvet and wood-paneled walls. There was even a couple of wait staffers, dressed in formal clothes, who attended to the distinguished guests of the carriage and who seemed to hold themselves in high esteem, if not for their own sake, then for the sake of those whom they served.

Cezal went to the bar, got a drink, and wandered around a bit before coming upon a table with Dzhes and another man and woman who all seemed to be engaged in interesting conversation. Dzhes spotted Cezal and waved him over with the unique eagerness of those who think themselves charming in their inebriation.

"If I may interrupt you for a moment, dear Molem," Dzhes broke in as Cezal arrived, putting his arms on his shoulders as he introduced him. "This is my old friend Ebem, with whom I read geometry in Bjumme."

"Pleasure to meet you, Ebem."

"Likewise," replied Cezal.

Molem sniffed.

"Yes, so," Molem continued, "as I was saying, indeed I do flaunt my wealth. I wear expensive clothes, waste my money on tropical houses, and just generally cultivate the emptiness and boredom that only the ultrarich have the privilege of basking in." He looked over at Cezal, who stood squeezed around the cocktail table between a middle-aged woman and man, both dressed rather smartly. "We come from a place where money is virtuous and righteous—you all understand." He seemed to have spoken directly to Cezal to clarify that last point. "I flaunt it, knowing there are those who need it far more than do I. 'There will come a time, sooner or later, when there will be a revolution and the wealth will be redistributed.' Hah! How many times in history could people utter that phrase? What a quaint sentiment that is—framing the world as though it's all or nothing. And while the lessers are preoccupied with their dithery and egalitarianism, we enjoy ourselves. And regardless, even if there were some revolution, those fuckheads don't understand their world or themselves well enough to actually change anything. All they'd do is change the figureheads."

He took a sip of his drink and shrugged. "But I digress. Perhaps it will happen. I suppose it's bound to happen at *some* point. And when, or rather *if*, that time comes," Molem continued, a twinkle in his eye, "I will be taken by a mob from my decadent life and have a rope tied on my foot. I will be hung from one of the many baroque gables on my estate swinging upside down, frantically trying to get out—screaming in desperation as I have never screamed before. Ready to grovel as I have never groveled before. The lessers will come and shower me with rotten food, with spit, with piss and smear shit in my mouth and face." And he waved his meaty hand violently over his face with a smirk. "They will bludgeon me, with their tools, with their righteous fists, and I will scream and holler with panic and plead for their pity and clemency. But they will laugh in my face and savor killing me all the more."

He paused and made sure to look at everyone at the table right in the eye. "But I will not, for even one second in my desperation, regret the life I have lived. No."

He shook his head before continuing, "For it is I who is truly righteous!" He waved his arms as he said that. "For *I* am the martyr of decadence! I am of the few among us who is honest. I may flaunt my wealth, but I am far from the only one. The rest of our lot pretend to care about the poor but still live their lives, making sure they never have to see a homeless person. Who is it that said the devil's greatest trick was convincing the world he didn't exist? Well, there you go."

He shrugged and took a sip of his martini. "So fuck them. And fuck me. At the very least, I have the dignity to spit in the face of those who are lower than I. And if that doomed *revolution* comes, they will be rightfully kill me in a torrent of hate and fury and poetic justice. Yes," he repeated more slowly, "At least I am honest. For none who truly know the weight I bear would want to be me. Many deify me, and many spit at the mere sight of my name in a newspaper. People hold such hate for me, for it is I who embodies the decrepitude of this gilded age. It is I who gets that near-sublime honor, and I bask in it. But in the end, I respect and hate the lessers to equal degrees. And for that reason, I am right. I am righteous. What a world it is, eh?" And he flashed Cezal a playful smile with a glimmer in his eye. "Really, Ebem, you should be *thanking* me for my sacrifice."

Their ensuing laughter bounced off the walls. Cezal watched them all with their terrible expressions, looking at the table as though out-of-body. He considered how much longer he should wait before making his excuses to return to his cabin. He decided he would leave the table but figured it would be rude to leave Dzhes so soon and instead settled for enjoying a drink on his own in one of the overstuffed chairs toward the back. That was indeed a luxury he had been missing after sitting so long on either the floor or the foot of his bed.

By then, it was completely dark outside. There was nothing really to see through the window, but for the part of the ground closest to the train illuminated by the inside lights.

Later, the woman he had been standing next to at the cocktail table walked over to Cezal and stood by the chair opposite to him.

"Is this seat free?"

Cezal motioned that it was, and she sat down.

"You're probably wondering what the deal with all this talk of money and righteousness is about, eh?"

Cezal looked at her and did his best to hide his less-than-cordial feelings toward them all.

"Mm, yes, I suppose," he began. "I must admit, this isn't quite my milieu. I've come to sit here to get a break from all the rather ostentatious talk. Certainly, you agree that guy, Molem, is being rather over-the-top, or?" Cezal looked at her, trying to probe to seem more at ease.

She threw her head up and laughed. "Oh, I *know*. That's just how he is. I wouldn't take it the wrong way. But, in the spirit of adventure, perhaps I'll overshare a bit." She leaned in and put on the face one has when relaying superficially serious information but cares more about the reaction of whom one speaks to than the actual information itself. "You see," she paused for effect, "Molem over there just had *quite* the controversy. For the sake of protecting his privacy, I won't tell you much of the specifics, but he's quite high up in the company he works for and was recently caught having a bit more fun with the profits than one should and was on trial for 'Misappropriation of Capital,' as the court took to calling it. Ah, but he came out okay. You know how these things work out." She took a sip of her drink—a gin and tonic by the looks of it. "But anyway, he's now in the proverbial doghouse, so he's been sent to deal with some issues in the East."

"I see." Cezal nodded. "So who are you then?"

She tilted her head to the side and gave a sly smile. "I, well, I'm an asset manager of sorts. For now, though, let's just say I stick around him to make sure he doesn't get into more trouble." She glanced over to the table where the rest of them were still carrying on. "It's interesting to see him like this, though, I must admit. He's normally the kind of person who seems so composed." She made a composure-evoking gesture with her free hand as she said it—drawing her fingers together similarly to how an actor does after saying "and scene." "But," she continued, "I suppose it really has shaken him up. I've never seen him squirm before like he did during the trial. Tell me, have you seen someone who seemed so powerful and infallible truly *squirm*, truly think the jig's up?"

Cezal shook his head. "I can't say I have."

"Well," she gave a lightly throaty laugh, "let me tell you, it's a very humanizing experience. And now, when I hear Molem talk, I'm able to see what he's really trying to do, with his projections of guilt and his this and that. That's the funny thing—he got off, but he knows what he did, and he's still feeling the heat. He used to always seem so sure of himself, though. I guess no one is above their own consciousness, or in his case, paranoia."

"Hm, I suppose not." Cezal replied, nodding lightly, "But what do you think of what he said—about an ill-fated revolution and his self-proclaimed martyrdom?"

"Oh *that*," she chuckled. "Well, I mean, it's bullshit, of course. Like I said—he's just projecting his paranoia, just saying what he wants to be true, hoping if he does it enough, he'll actually believe it. And hey, there'll probably be a handsome number of schmucks who've got their heads so far up his ass they'll believe it too." She paused for a few seconds. "Perhaps I should let you in on a little secret," and she gave a subtly patronizing smile and nod of the head. "I decided long ago I wouldn't bind myself to unnecessary morals. Or that, at the very least, I would be completely honest with myself about what I really was. I was born rich. I had 'privilege,' if you wish to so call it, in every imaginable way. Ah, and how

I have come to embrace it. I know I'm a pariah. But you can see I need not care about it. I find other people like me. We have our nice cocktail parties," she added, gesturing around the train car. "Some of us pretend to care about immigrants, about homelessness, about undue stigma. Ha! But oh, I love it nonetheless. It's a show, you know, of course." And she took a sip of her drink while nodding. "Anyone who actually cared about any of those things wouldn't just feel bad and commiserate over it at brunch. They would actually act—and throwing a charity gala doesn't count! I considered this in my early adulthood. I saw the self-deception these people were engaged in, this doublethink, to make them feel morally just while doing next to nothing about it. I thought, what is the difference between them and a person who simply is honest with themselves about how they don't give a shit about starvation or racial injustice, or whatever the fuck it is that's en vogue to care about? Nothing! And so I've lived my life. I'm *amoral*."

She raised both arms and lightly shook her hands. "Woo, what formidable words those are. Yes. And I know I could have cared, but alas the poor, the destitute, the suffering— they're simply not me." She looked at Cezal's rather surprised face. "'But justice! But karma!' You cry. Hah, what justice? If there were justice, they wouldn't have been born with a system that works against them, and I wouldn't have been born with a silver spoon. As for karma? Say whatever you want about it. I've decided that if something does come to bite me in the end, I will look back regretting nothing. And if I do? Well, tough luck for me, I guess. Oh well. Until then, the party goes on…" She shrugged her shoulders and gave a cheeky smile. "But regardless, I've talked far too loosely. Though I have a strong suspicion, you're neither Dzhes' 'old friend' nor anyone of high enough status to be of any threat to us."

She looked at Cezal's mouth, slightly agape, trying to think of how to reply. She kept talking before he could articulate a thought. "Don't take that the wrong way. My filter's been gone a long time, so I'm just saying what immediately comes to mind. But anyhow, I think Molem's calling me back over. It was nice talking to you… Ebem." And off she sauntered to mingle with the other guests in the dinner cart after giving Cezal a raised eyebrow and a wink.

And Cezal was left to sit there. Despite the late hour, the party was hardly beginning to die down. There was still plenty raucous laughter to be heard, and loud phrases yelled between tables. The scenery outside would have looked the same as it had when he was in the dining car, though he could no longer see the vague silhouettes of trees from earlier. The inside was too bright and the outside too dark, so the windows simply acted as mirrors.

A waiter came over and offered him a gin and tonic, which he reluctantly accepted, taking to sipping on it while idly watching the corporate fauna play their games. His old companion, Dzhes, looking much worse for wear, came to sit with him, letting out a haggard sigh and sloppily putting his arm around Cezal as he picked up the chair and moved it closer to Cezal's.

"Oh, Ebem," Dzhes began, "look what we've become. Look at this." He began to weep a bit and draped himself awkwardly over Cezal. "I… I think I'm a bad person, Ebem," he said, half-muttering into Cezal's armpit. "I want not to be, but I think I am." He looked up at Cezal. "But you justify me, Ebem. You help make me feel more human. That's why I love you. Thank you." He stayed in that draped position for a few more moments, listening to Cezal's consistent breathing and heartbeat before sitting up and wiping his eyes. "Heh." Dzhes said after sniffing, "Well, this does bring us back to our night's in Bjumme, eh Ebem? Ah, those were the days, weren't they?"

Cezal smiled half-heartedly, figuring he needn't put too much care into keeping up airs. "Indeed they were, Dzhes. Indeed they were."

Not too long later, Cezal left to go to sleep.

* * *

The next morning, Cezal, as usual, took his tea and breakfast of rye toast and butter with Iljantva in their quaint cabin. It wasn't until nearly three in the morning when he had gotten to sleep. She noted his sluggishness shortly after he walked back in, two cups of breakfast tea in tow. He explained what had happened and the rather unpleasant people he had met, including in his recounting, of course, how his stint at being Ebem went.

"Well, it sounds like you sat at the right dinner booth last night, eh?" she said with a wink.

Cezal laughed. "Well, yes, one could say that."

They then proceeded to eat and made the pleasant conversation that one would make on such a morning. After a while, Cezal finished and leaned back, pulling out the local newspaper they sold at the breakfast canteen. At that point, it was really more of a weekly gazette filled with the sparse goings-on in the region. With so few people, not too much was happening. All the action was in the capital or the other major cities. Regardless, it was something to read. He sat back a bit on the bed, his back against the wall and his leg crossed casually over the other.

"Is there anything interesting in there?" Iljantva asked after she finished her meal.

He shook his head. "Oh, nothing out of the ordinary. There are a lot of horses running around after the caretaker fell asleep while bringing them back up north."

"Oh really?" She began to look wistfully at the wall behind Cezal. "You know, my older brother, Velden, being the kind never to live according to someone else's agenda, left home at sixteen to be a caretaker of horses."

"Is that so?" inquired Cezal, putting down the gazette and uncrossing his legs so he could lean forward.

"Yes." Iljantva nodded. "And it fit him too. He was always one for the open road. Farming would never have been suitable for him. He used to come back to visit every fall and brought with him some gift from a far-off place that always seemed so foreign. I remember a book once he brought that had such far-out stories, written in a strange dialect I often had a hard time understanding. They were folktales or something of the like, but the tone in them was always so fantastical and dreamy." She leaned back, her hand rubbing her chin. "There was one about a mermaid who came to live on land but grew increasingly lonely and returned to the sea, only to realize her kingdom was gone. That one was especially sad in the end because she had built so much of her life on land, having married and established herself in her town, you wondered why she was going back, and of course, then she did, and found nothing…" Iljantva sighed. "Ah, but it brings back memories."

"Were you close with him?" Cezal asked.

"Oh," Iljantva paused, looking back at Cezal after having drifted off in memory, "No. I mean, how could we have been? He came only for about a month every September or October.

But it was nice when he was there. I always saw him as this strong, fiercely free figure. It's nice to have looked up to your older brother, no?"

"Yes, I imagine it would be," Cezal replied with a light smile.

"Do you have any siblings, Cezal?"

"No," he replied, "It was always my mother and me for as long as I can remember. As one would imagine, it was rather quiet growing up." He nodded. "But it was nice."

Iljantva grunted kindly in agreement, and they sat for some time in silence, listening to the rhythmic clack of the train and enjoying the morning sun streaming in through the window, softly warming their skin.

"I don't want to sound obsessive, but I keep going over last night in my head," Cezal replied some moments later.

Iljantva looked over. "What about it?"

"Well, just the way they were so sure about themselves and how slimy it all was."

She smiled. "What is it about that that bothers you?"

"I don't know exactly," he replied. "It just felt wrong."

"Well," began Iljantva, "they're certainly not the kind of people whom I'd want to have over for Sunday brunch. But your initial feelings aside, the question is, 'do you think they're right?'" She looked him directly in the eyes while asking that last bit.

Cezal stared back and then looked away—out, through the window. "I… well, I don't know. I can't help but feel like they're just *wrong* on some basic level."

"And do you think they'll get away with it?" she probed.

Cezal gave a reproachful scoff. "I mean, I guess so. But how is that okay?"

"It's not," she replied. "But what is one to do about it?"

"Well, you can't just accept it, can you?"

"You don't have to, no. But it doesn't really get you any-where," she replied, her frankness ringing through the small cabin.

"How can you say that?"

"How?" She raised her eyebrows, "Because I speak from experience. It's not to say you should never 'fight the power.' No. But to simply get upset with them is a waste of emotional energy, don't you think? And many times, people are encour-aged to 'fight the power,' but aren't given any real tools to do so, so they resort to means of fighting that may feel good in the short-term but ultimately serve as little more than an emotional release."

"So we should just accept our powerlessness?"

"No. That's not what I mean." Iljantva clarified, "We should be honest with ourselves, and see that we don't have the proper tools to deal with what we're trying to deal with and accept that we're wasting our breath. My time is over to try to change such things, so I don't let it bother me, but for the youth, it's not."

She paused a moment and rubbed her chin. "I hear myself, and I can tell I'm out of touch. Only those who don't really suffer at the hand of injustice would be so dismissive. Make of it what you will." She sniffed. "That said, authentic-ity, especially authenticity with the self, is an undervalued trait nowadays. That's what's needed for true growth and change. That's what's needed to make the proper tools for creating meaningful change. Maybe it sounds overly sim-plified when I put it this way, but it's just to say you can't properly change what you can't properly see and understand. You must perceive yourself before you can change the world around you."

"I suppose you make a good point. But then do you mean to say they are justified in doing what they do?" Cezal asked.

"No." She shook her head. "I don't mean that. But I think you mix up the things we say exist with the things we want to exist. I do my best to have no illusions about the world, Cezal. I have seen time and time again that there is no justice, no higher ideal, nothing: they're pleasant fictions…" She coughed. "But I shouldn't sound so cynical. Those things need to be fought for. Otherwise, they will fade into existence like a forgotten story, and we'll suffer until we learn those lessons again the hard way. And *that's* the point," she added with emphasis. "If we want justice, or freedom, or whatever right, it has to be fought for. If we take it for granted and think of it as something that exists outside of ourselves, as though some universal principle, then we're setting ourselves up for terrible things."

Cezal nodded, and they both sat in silence for a while. The intensity and angle of the sun accentuated Iljantva's wrinkles.

"I have seen amazing acts in my life—people never cease to surprise you. But at the same time, I feel like nothing much ever changes. Perhaps it's the people that do," she mused. "And I don't mean on a big scale, but on the individual level. For example, the hopeful youth, the anti-establishment, they grow up and become themselves the defenders of the world order. And then, the youth look at the old curmudgeons they have for parents and swear they won't be like them, so stuck in their ways, and then scare themselves as they get older once they have their own children and suddenly hear the words of their mother or father spoken out of their own mouth. That's a rather small example," she admitted, "but it applies on the wider scale. Things have a way of changing on the surface, but in the end, it's all the same stuff. We don't have any different problems than people did one hundred or even a thousand years ago—at least not really. It's rather funny the way things go. You'll start to notice patterns in how people live their lives and whom they become. Often, they'll become the very things they hate the most. Not necessarily in a bitter way—though that certainly is a possibility—but it's to say that opposites have a way of becoming the other." She paused a bit and looked out the window at the passing trees glimmering in the sun. "We have the tendency to forget the reason we do things. We confound the journey with the destination, the method with the intended result. That's how we get out of touch with ourselves. No point in getting down about it. It's simply how it is, and it's best to keep oneself aware of it."

She shrugged her shoulders at Cezal in a what-can-you-do kind of way, and they both sat for a bit in silence, listening to the train clack.

"I see," Cezal replied. "So what do you suggest?"

"What do I suggest for you?" Iljantva asked.

"Well, I suppose."

She gave a wry smile and chuckled. "I wish I had a good answer. All I can say for sure is that the beginning of the 'solution' will be found in first changing yourself. Your environment will come to reflect that change. And the importance of the community too—we can't ignore that. That's certainly an aspect of society that we, in the modern world, have forgotten the importance of. Perhaps, it would be accurate to consider our lives like community gardens and we, the gardeners. It takes hard and consistent effort to have a healthy garden, and there are many external factors outside of our control that can affect the quality of our gardens and their crops. But at the end of the day, we must feed ourselves with the fruits and vegetables from those gardens, regardless of whatever fortune or misfortune may befall us. That is perhaps the best attitude for life that I can suggest. Cultivate your gardens as best as possible and help others in their efforts as well."

3

———

"You know, Cezal," began Iljantva the next day while they were both sitting and reading. "I have been thinking about what you said about those businesspeople the other day. They all had a rather healthy amount of arrogance, didn't they?"

Cezal looked up from his book. "Well, that's one way to put it," he chuckled.

"Mm, well, I wonder," began Iljantva. "If there *were* some kind of 'justice,' it would perhaps act in the way that those who are bad are bad out of their own shortsightedness and so create their own downfall."

"How do you mean?"

"Well, if there's one thing that seems like a constant, it's that arrogance will always lead to one's downfall. It is, in my experience, one of the most destructive emotions—especially when it arises out of a hurt ego. That is why they say anger, more often than not, is a hurt ego masked in fire. So be very careful with it. Ego is what gets in the way of perceiving reality and what needs to be done to achieve your goal. It distorts and blinds. It makes you see things that aren't there or pay attention to the inconsequential. Our downfall will always come about in an unexpected way and will always arise due to the causes we ourselves make. That is why we must always be vigilant with ourselves." She shrugged. "And didn't those people seem diluted and misguided?"

"Yes," Cezal replied.

"And yet, they were, by most metrics, rather smart people, no?" Iljantva asked.

"I would assume so," he replied.

She shrugged. "Well, I feel like it would be a fair assessment to say it's their arrogance that has debased them and caused them to lose sight of what is important."

"I suppose so," Cezal replied. "But how can we say they really are in the wrong if, as you say, morality and justice and all that are just stories we tell ourselves?"

Iljantva shook her head. "You misunderstand what I meant. You only have justice insofar as you do just actions. Those stories of justice and higher ideals give us a template to base our lives around but don't exist independently of ourselves. So while they most likely won't suffer any consequences from a retributive perspective, they're almost certain to be unhappy. Regardless of whether one agrees or not, it is the value we create in our lives that matters in the end. And by this, I don't mean the value of wealth or the desire to live a life at ease, but rather the life to be found in introspection and self-overcoming and truly respecting other people. The older you get, the more you come to see how transient so many of the things we think are important actually are. That is why we old people seem so simple and lonely—most of them, or rather us, have come to see our mortality. Many have realized we had always had the wrong priorities and so are stuck steeping in regret, lamenting the futility of it all."

They sat in silence for a while, staring outside of the window, admiring the scenery while Cezal mulled over her words.

"And at the same time, though, truly knowing what really matters is such a cherishable and pure thing. It's really the best gift one could receive or give. How wonderful it is we live in a world where we can make someone else feel loved and cherished, and to think someone could do the same for you!" She gave a kind smile to Cezal before looking out the window again.

* * *

One of the often less-appreciated aspects of the train trip is the people watching it afforded. Due to the heat of the train, many people kept their cabin doors open for more circulation. Because of the general lack of privacy, it was so easy to look out the window and watch nature while over-hearing the family from three cabins down. It was, however, a benefit not lost on Cezal, who enjoyed watching people as they lived their lives: who it was that woke the earliest and who got tea for the rest of the cabin; the old man in the ragged and drab, but always clean, clothes who would sit around reading his novels or the paper; the crying babies; the stifling heat—those who seemed more comfortable with it and those who simply sweat through their clothes and who stood in front of the window to feel the little slit of air that would come in from being able to lower the top part slightly; those who were preoccupied with work and were annoyed with living in such close quarters with others; and those who seemed to appreciate the high concentration of humanity. Like a never-ending tapestry of the mundane, the days went by.

"You look like the kind of person who is able to wonder at the small things, no?" Iljantva asked on one such day.

Cezal looked at her, startled out of his daydreaming. "Uh, well, yes, I suppose. I've never really thought about it."

"Well, it's a good skill to have. It's certainly one that's underrated," she added.

"Are you able to wonder at the small things, Iljantva?" Cezal asked, sitting forward as she sat up and scootched to the foot of her bed to sit and face him.

"Yes, I think so, though it gets easier the older you get. But yes, it's nice, isn't it?"

"Mm, yes it is," he replied.

They both people watched and enjoyed the late summer views of the forest for a while. The gently sloping hills and the endless pine trees interrupted by the occasional clearing. Every once in a while, a small hut with smoke rising out the top, probably preparing lunch, was seen, often with a dwarf-like horse or two never far away.

"Do you think most people feel trapped by their life, Iljantva?" Cezal mused, sitting back, his legs crossed in the nonchalant way they often seemed to be in as of late.

She looked back at him and took a moment to think.

"Probably," she replied. "I don't think most people really know themselves or really care to either. They come to be satisfied with where they are because that's what they're used to."

"And what does this result in?" Cezal asked.

"Well, a quiet dissatisfaction, I would say. I think it eats at some people more than others though," she replied.

"Why do you think this is?"

Iljantva turned her head from the window to look at Cezal and smiled. "Why do *you* think this is, Cezal?"

He paused and smiled himself. "Oh, well, I suppose it's a coping mechanism of sorts, isn't it? Coping with what exactly, I don't know—their own life, or perhaps themselves. Most people, I suppose, are disappointed on some level with what they've become and who they are."

Iljantva nodded and thought for some time. "I think you're right. It's natural and necessary to look for ways to cope. Some of them are maladaptive, and some not, but they allow for us to function. I don't say this in a good or bad way, but simply to explain it. I've come to see that most of all, though, what people want is to have a sense of belonging. If they can't find it in community or their family, they look for it in other areas. Especially nowadays, in our times of alienation and baselessness, people feel the need to supplement a lack of a sense-of-self with other things, be it their job, a role in society, ideologies, the way they dress, nationalism, or even something as mundane, in the West, as astrology and horoscopes. We all tell ourselves stories to define ourselves by." She paused to let Cezal process the words before continuing. "There is the *story* we have of ourselves and the story we have within our family and friends. The dynamic changes all the time, depending on whom we're with. It's a narrative we tell to ourselves about who we are and what the world is, like a self-written script for life—and it's one we're usually only half-conscious of! I am an *honorable* person or I am loyal or I am disgusting. They're all quaint stories, and none of them are any more or less real than another."

She paused for a rare deep breath—her ability to go on speaking without pause being a unique feat for someone her age. "Or really, that's most likely what it is. We all have basic beliefs of ourselves that can, many times, be summed up in a single sentence, but most people don't know themselves, or rather, their self-written story, well enough to name even one of those beliefs. The reason I say this is because there are many who seem to think people can't change, or at least not really." She took another breath and looked at Cezal's expression to try to discern what he was thinking about this. "Now, I'm no optimist," she continued. "I do my best not to say things simply because I like the way they sound or make me feel, but nor am I a pessimist. If someone truly wishes to recon with oneself, then it's possible to do so. Everyone is only circumstantially bound to the person they see themselves as—to the person they were yesterday, to the person they were a decade ago. In the end, it's all simply a story. Do with it what you wish."

She paused again, leaving time for Cezal to mull over her words more. The beauty of the summer was indeed something to wonder at—something that never got old. And the summers of the north were different than those further south. Perhaps it was because it was dark and cold for so much of the year that the people and animals and flowers and trees simply appreciated it more and glowed brighter in the midnight sun for it.

Iljantva began again, "To speak on those people you saw on the train the other day in context to what I've just said… well, to speak frankly, those are simply not the kinds of people one should waste one's time having high expectations of. They are the most comfortable. Just as that woman who knew you weren't Ebem said, they themselves are the ones who benefit most from the way things are. At least they were honest. There are far more people like them who pretend to be against *the system*, and gain wider acceptance because of it, but when it comes time for *real* change, they're nowhere to be found." She shrugged. "Ah, but who should be surprised? When it comes down to it, Cezal, most people don't care about the righteous things they claim to care about enough to actually bring their self-proclaimed beliefs into reality."

"You think so?" he asked, looking almost hurt by what she just said.

"Well, yes, I do," she replied. "We live in a world in which there are haves and have-nots. Those who have, understandably, want to keep it that way. In our times, there are two main arguments the haves make. They either do their best to create moral justification for having what they have, such were the people you met the other day, or they claim to be on the side of the have-nots while not doing much to actually make the have-nots *have*. The people who are on the first side are the easy ones to dislike. They come off, rightfully, as arrogant and self-righteous, and one learns quickly not to give them the time of day. The other group, however, is more subtle. Most of them don't even admit to themselves they are part of the problem. They think they're on the side of the righteous, but in this way, they are perhaps even more insincere than the group that openly vilifies the have-nots! And after all, it's much easier to sleep at night when you think you're the victim. To realize that, in fact, *you* are among the *evildoers* is a much harder truth to accept. In this way, those obnoxious people you met on the train car are perhaps the more sincere ones. At least they are honest with themselves. Of course, that doesn't actually change anything, but at least they don't pretend to be anything they're not. But yes, they seem like they're a rather sickening, overly vulgar lot. I certainly wouldn't want to spend my time with them, but it was an interesting experience, nonetheless, wouldn't you say?"

"Yes, an interesting experience is one way to put it. And I suppose that's true, what you say about their authenticity. But those who are brazen in their lack of regard for the world—are they just as bad as those who pretend to care?" Cezal asked.

"Just as bad?" Iljantva asked. "I think in their sincerity, they'd be considered better. I'm even inclined to have some sort of respect for them. Those who aren't honest with themselves are weak, Cezal. They can be manipulated and made to do almost anything. That's why there are all these ideologues trying to start this movement here or push that narrative there, running around thinking they're the next messiah. And who knows? Maybe some of them will be successful. Only time will tell if they come to be seen as such." She paused a moment to smack her lips. "But that's the thing—those people you met last night, no ideologue will ever sway them, even a truly righteous one. Those people already have their money and power. That gives them enough. We like to deride the weak, but with weak people, you know even if their heart isn't in the right place initially, you can make them do good. But with the so-called *strong*, well, if their heart isn't in the right place, there's not much you can do."

Cezal raised his eyebrows and wasn't sure if he agreed or not. "What does that mean then?" he asked. "That you just have to hope there are enough strong people with their hearts in the right place?"

"Certainly not," Iljantva replied. "Though that is a part of it. Like I said before, it's all just stories we have of ourselves. If weak people chose to be strong, then they can be strong. If people chose to be evil then they can be evil. That's why it's important we be honest with ourselves. That's why sincerity is a step in the right direction."

Cezal nodded, and they sat in silence for a while.

"If I'm being honest, Cezal," Iljantva broke in, "I can't claim to call myself good either. I help perpetuate the system, as people seem to like to call it. I am a have." She looked at him, trying to read his expression. "I can see, you're looking at me guiltily. You see yourself as being more of a have than I do, eh? Well, I can't argue with your conclusion, Cezal. But what is one to do? Self-flagellation? Bah. Guilt, in most cases, is another form of self-importance. Let it spur change in how you act, but don't let it get to you. But anyhow, yes, I think it's fair to say I'm part of this morally decrepit era. Most people are."

"But," Cezal furrowed his eyebrows, "where does that leave us?"

"Where does it leave us, Cezal? I really don't know. Most people are a disappointment. I'm no exception. Now, let's not be simpleminded. There are a million shades of good and bad and a million different ways of helping or hurting the world. It does little good to try and add all this up mathematically or to say only those who have sacrificed their entire lives for the greater good are themselves good and the rest of us lamentable beings. No, I know I'm not on the same level as those people you met last night, and I, and hopefully you as well, know better than to conflate us two with them. But I also know I'm only comfortable enough with my moral decrepitude because I face no real consequences for it. What little I can perhaps say is that the least one can do is make sure to treat others with respect—consider them to be valid people with valid feelings. It's easy to feel powerless to big systems, but we have a lot more control over our environments than we think. And no matter who you are, you can always change the way you interact with others for the better. Perhaps that's a rather paltry response, but that is the best I, or anyone else I've come across, can offer."

Cezal stared at her for a bit.

"You look disillusioned with me, Cezal. I know you look up to me and like to hear my advice, but no one is ever more than human. We're all hypocrites."

She gave him a light smile, and he nodded. They sat the rest of the time just staring out the window of the train as the pine trees whipped by. It was comfortable. Not too much later, it was lunchtime.

* * *

Sometime after lunch, the afternoon sun was filtering through the trees and turning the forest a golden orange hue, and Cezal was laying down half-asleep with a brown felted hat on his face to block the sun. Iljantva began to muse out loud, her hands clasped neatly on the table. "You know, Cezal, I'd like to think if I only had a little bit of time left before I die, I'd accept it gracefully. And at my age, I feel like that's becoming less and less of a theoretical. But when I imagined being told I only had a few months left to live, I imagine myself saying 'oh,' because, of course, what really is there to say? But then I imagine feeling perhaps a certain disappointment because I'll realize I don't think I've felt like my life has really started yet."

"How do you mean?" Cezal asked, taking the hat off his face to look at Iljantva.

"Well, I suppose I feel like I'm at the theater and I'm waiting for the show to start, and in the meantime, I've been chatting with the people around me and not having a half-bad time either, all things considered. But I'm still waiting for the curtain to draw. I don't know. Maybe there's been no curtain in the first place. Maybe I was just waiting for no reason."

The train clacked on, and the sun streamed warmly through the window.

"I suppose so, but you still had your friends and pleasant time waiting," Cezal replied, still laying down.

She shrugged. "Yes, it's nice, but I must admit, it's a bit of a letdown. I suppose right now, I'm asking myself what it would take for me to feel like the curtain *has* risen, or perhaps to realize the curtain rose the second I was born."

Cezal was unsure how to respond.

"I suppose it has already risen, hasn't it," he decided to say. "A rather tedious play we're in then, isn't it?"

She chuckled.

"Yes, I suppose the exposition has dragged on a bit, hasn't it?" she added. "Other times, though, I feel like I've been around for so long and seen and experienced so much. I feel like I've been alive forever."

"Well, isn't that how we all feel? It's hard to conceive of a time before you existed," Cezal replied.

She tilted her head lightly and gave a gentle smile. "Well, yes, I suppose that's true, but it's different when you're older. You look back, and it's almost as if you can hold the time in your hand, and the older you get, the more you come to be able to hold. You come to spend a lot of time looking through the memories you've accumulated. I don't know how else to say it, but when you do that, you feel a special sorrow for what once was. And you know, sometimes it's nice because I have all those parts of me inside—all those people I once was. Perhaps then, it could be said that I still am them," she sighed. "Memories are a nice thing, Cezal. They really are. I feel like worlds that have died and will never return still live on in my memories, and that truly is a marvel." She nodded resolutely. "It really makes you cherish the past and the present."

The conversation trailed on for a bit after that, and eventually, Cezal nodded off again, and she took to looking out the window at the trees dancing in their afternoon light. She stayed there, staring until there was only enough light to make of the pine trees a never-ending silhouette decorating what was left of the red and purple sky. Some handful of hours later, the sun would rise again.

4

The honey light of late summer was inviting, and it was early enough that the crisp morning air was still coming in through the barely cracked upper window. The clacks and pleasant whistle of the wind decorated the amber covered cabin. Iljantva was sitting on the bed, at the table drinking her tea and looking out the window at the scenery—the seemingly never-ending forest, punctuated by the occasional clearing. Every once in a while, they passed a clearing with goats or sheep, gazing disinterestedly at the train as it chugged past. Cezal laid on his back on the bed, awake, but with his arm over his eyes to block out the sun, enjoying the crisp air and the train's rhythm.

"Cezal, I have a thought experiment for you," said Iljantva, who had already eaten and just finished her morning tea.

He took his arm off his face and groggily sat up, curiosity piqued.

"Oh?" asked Cezal a moment later as he got situated, leaning on their table with both elbows.

"Well," she began, "in light of our discussions about people, I thought it would be good to try and get to know yourself better. It's a rather tactless way of asking you, perhaps, but it's an important enough matter that it's worth cutting your half-sleep short. My question is a simple one—probably one that, in one form or another, you had contemplated quite a bit when you were younger. Who do you think you would be if all of the things that make you *you* were taken away?"

"What exactly do you mean?" he asked.

"Well," she replied, taking a deep breath in, "I assume you have a certain conception of yourself. Just like we've talked about before."

"Mm… yes, I suppose."

"What do you mean 'suppose,' Cezal? We talked about this just a couple of days ago. Did you apply the concept to yourself?"

"Oh, well, I felt like I've been considering it thoroughly," he replied, "though I suppose I haven't really applied it to myself."

"Okay, well, so what happens when you do apply it to yourself?"

He thought for a bit and shifted his weight, so he was resting more toward the window.

"I suppose I get that I see of myself as a banker, as a son, a member of my town—no one too exciting, but reliable nonetheless." He paused and shifted to look more out the window before continuing. "I see myself as level-headed. I try not to let things get to me, and I put things in perspective. I guess you could say I consider myself rather stoic."

"I see," she said. "And what would you do if your background were taken away from you?"

Cezal furrowed his eyebrows. "How do you mean taken away?"

"Well, consider you were a farmer instead of a banker and that you grew up, accordingly, on a farm, you married relatively young, had many siblings, and were somewhat hot-headed. Who would you *be* then?"

"I think it's one thing to change my background, but another to change my personality, for example, by saying I'd be hotheaded," he countered. "That's not something which can be taken away because it doesn't rely on circumstance."

She nodded slowly. "Well, I think you're right," she admitted, "I'll amend that then: you've been made a farmer and live the farmer lifestyle. Save the personality questions for later and consider just that. Who would you *be* in this case?"

He smiled a bit as he thought. "Well, someone else, I suppose." He glanced into his empty teacup from the day before.

"Perhaps. But do you see though how that *could* have been your life, were you born into that?" Iljantva probed, leaning in and looking at him with playfully intense eyes.

"Well… yes," he admitted.

"And do you see how, if somehow you bumped your head and managed to forget your entire life up to now and thought instead that you were a farmer, that you'd be very different?"

"Yes," he began nodding slowly. "But that's rather a different question altogether. Had I been *born* a farmer, that would have changed my life experiences, and thus my conception of the world, and it's *that* which would have shaped my personality. To simply think of myself as a farmer wouldn't change anything in the present. I would understand my relationship with society and the world in a different way, so I would only react to things differently in the future. That is what would change my personality."

Iljantva nodded pensively. "That's a good point. But that said, because there is that *potential* in you, or there *was* that potential in you, can you say that there's really any inherent difference between you and the farmer, or you and anyone else for that matter?"

Cezal didn't say anything for a bit. "Well, that's a difficult thing to just agree to outright. I see your logic, but I'm not sure."

"That's quite understandable," Iljantva replied. "In the meantime, though, my dear, what I'm trying to get you to see is that people are ideas. Very beautiful, complex ideas, sure, but ideas nonetheless. Would you not say so?" She paused, waiting for a response, but continued when he didn't change his expression. "Because we consider and apply this image of who we think we are to ourselves, but then we must apply that same way of thinking to our conceptions of others. When we do that, we realize other people are just that—conceptions that exist only in our mind."

"So you're saying that not only are we just empty narratives, but other people are also empty narratives?" Cezal asked.

"In a manner of speaking, yes. We and other people are empty narratives. *But*, the important thing is, our narratives of them are going to be different than their own narratives of themself. What I'm saying is there is nothing essential to the human identity, but nonetheless, we think of ourselves as being real, static beings. Then, when we look at other people, not only do we see them as real, static beings, but when we try to get to know them, we think we are getting to know who the other person is, but really, we're just forming our own conception of them."

He furrowed his eyebrows. "So what does that mean?"

"Well, it has many implications. But basically, it means that there is no real you that exists, and in the same way, there is no way to know the real me because I also don't exist—at least not in some concrete way."

Cezal stared at her for a bit and then out the window, at the endlessly passing trees and the occasional railroad marker.

"Well," he said, looking back over, "I'll have to give that more thought."

Iljantva nodded but still had more to say. "I do want to add, though, I think there is the trap people fall into when they come to see we're nothing more to our identity than our self-conception. They start to think this means no one is real." She shrugged dismissively. "And I suppose that could be said, but people's obsession with the pure or true is most often terribly misguided. What people perhaps should consider more is that it is not people who are less real than we thought, but rather ideas which are more so than we thought."

"So ideas are people, you're saying?"

"No. Don't oversimplify what I'm trying to say," she said, shaking her head. "My point is simply that humans are closer to ideas than we think, and ideas are closer to being human than we think."

"How is this useful, though?" Cezal asked.

She paused a second and pushed her lips together while shrugging. "Well, there are many applications to be found, but in my experience, it's best to simply entertain a new concept for a while and mull over it; soon enough, you'll start to make connections automatically. But one thing I think can be useful is to consider our emotions, given they are concepts, as being more like people, and to think of ourselves as having a personal relationship with each one."

"Oh, well, that's certainly a nice point-of-view," Cezal replied.

"Yes," she replied back. "It is, and one that can give you strength in times when you lose hope."

"Ah, so is that why you've brought this thought experiment up?"

She smiled. "Well, in a roundabout way, I suppose. But try to keep yourself open to this way of thinking and really consider it before choosing whether or not to reject it."

"Okay, I will."

"I suppose," began Iljantva, "perhaps for your purposes, this is the application I think of: When we love another with our entire being, we love a conception. A relationship is a commitment that you will lament from time to time. There will be times when you don't feel love for your significant other, or friend, or whomever really, and in those times, we must commit ourselves to the relationship, understanding the value of a deep, well-cultivated connection. Well, the same can be said of love, beauty, hope, forgiveness, tenderness, and so on. They, too, are people with whom we are in a relationship. As such, we must give them our commitment, and in turn, so too will they commit to us. In a corresponding way, there too will come nights when you will be all alone, and you must whisper, as convincingly as possible to your friend hope that you love it and cherish it with your entire being, even when you feel like hope is nowhere to be found, and you'll never feel it again. As you say that, you must make yourself believe it. Otherwise, it will disappear, running off into the night never to be found. This is not some cheap trick I am telling you. I truly believe this. I know what I say is a bit unconventional, but please consider it. I think you will find life becomes much richer for it."

And he did consider it. They sat for a while, still facing each other on the maroon sheets, looking out the window at the nature of summer, with the trees and the occasional clearings. The big, blackbirds that would fly in their vee formation, probably toward a river somewhere, or latecomers to their summer home. The rare cottage with smoke coming out of the chimney and children playing around it. The light streamed in and painted their skin with warmth, and the world was indeed beautiful.

* * *

Earth tones met the dusky sky. The field felt endless, with neat rows of lavender blending into the horizon. At that time, the sun was setting, and the days were getting cooler. The afternoons were still hot, yes, but the coming fall had already taken out the most biting part of the heat. From a distance, riding in from the east came a man on a horse. The pitter-patter of feet on the floorboards and the throwing open of the front door onto to porch accompanied a happy shout: "Velden!"

Soon enough, he got his horse tied to the hitching post at the side of the house, and she ran up and hugged him.

"And how have you been, my dearest Janka?"

"Good," she replied, giggling. "What do you have in your bag?"

"Well, that's for later. In the meantime, let's say hi to Aunt."

From Velden's point of view, their aunt was the kind of person who often seemed too pleased with herself. Perhaps out of shallow confidence. Perhaps out of an inflated sense of importance. Or perhaps because she thought she'd amount to less than she had, but instead surpassed her expectations rather early on and got comfortable. All three of them were at dinner. She wore hearty, post-work linens, the same kind of which she made for Iljantva. They contrasted nicely with the rugged outfit of the modern-day cowboy who sat next to Iljantva, facing the door as always. Iljantva could see Velden's leather jacket on the hook by the door and loved it. These were the best times of the year. Her wonderful brother, so grand, so adventurous, and giving.

They sat around the table with their chicken and squash and wine. "So, Velden," the aunt began, leaning back in her chair after taking a bit sip of wine. "What have you been up to?"

Iljantva looked up at Velden, interested and happy to be included in the adult conversation around her.

"Well, you know how it is. The horses keep you busy. But you know," he said, turning to Iljantva with a smile, "just about a month ago, I got a new horse, quiet, but with a wonderful spirit. I haven't yet named her, but I thought maybe you, Janka, would like to name her? And then, next time I come back, I can bring with me the inventory list, stamped and official and all, and it will be your horse's name on there."

Iljantva smiled and put both her hands on the chair and swung her legs while swaying in her seat—as she used to always do when taken by the idea of something exciting. They waited a bit.

"Just think about it, and then get back to me, eh?" Velem said with a kind eye.

"You know, Velden, there's a new family a few farms down who need some help digging a well. Why don't I tell them you'll be able to give them a hand." She raised her eyebrow and played absentmindedly with her glass. "You *will* be staying long enough to help them with the well, won't you?"

Velden gave a tight smile and held in his annoyance at her lack of tact. "Yes, I should be here long enough to help with the well. I'll go over tomorrow morning and take a look."

"Ooh, could I come?" asked Iljantva.

He smiled at her. "Oh, I don't see why not. We can ride over together, eh? I assume you still remember my old horse."

"Of course I do!" she said, trying to look out the window at the horse even though it was already the deep, dark blue of the evening when anything you could see would only be a dark shadow barely discernable from the sky.

The aunt gave a short sniff and ate a bite of chicken. "Janka, dear. Eat your food. It's getting cold."

"It's okay," Iljantva replied. "It's already gotten cold." And she smiled innocently at Velden, who smiled back. The aunt gave no reply but stared only at her plate, fork loosely in hand.

"You're getting so much bigger every time I see you. You're almost at my elbows now!" Velden said, changing the subject.

"Well, yes, Velden," the aunt interjected. "That's what children do. They grow."

"Yes, well…," he replied half to her and half to Iljantva, "that is true, isn't it?" He winked. "Do you know what you want to do when you get older?"

She was going to say she wanted to be with him, with the horses. But she knew her aunt's disapproval of that, so she paused.

Her aunt chimed in. "I know what she wants to do," she said, tilting her head to Velden with an over-done bemusement. "She wants to be someone big and strong—someone who thinks they can save the world but leaves their responsibilities at home. To work with the horses—yes, Velden, she quite idolizes you. Perhaps, she even wants to be a sort of… heroic derelict, if one were to so romantically put it. I wonder where she got that from?"

Iljantva's eyebrow furrowed, and she tilted her chin down and looked at Velden. He laughed out of defensiveness. The aunt laughed out of resentment and mockery. Iljantva crumpled up and stared down at her cold chicken.

* * *

Cezal was sitting in his usual spot with a cup of barley tea, reading a letter from Miss Elmyta delivered to him at the last stop. She had sent a short note of the goings-on in the town.

Iljantva looked up disinterestedly from her crochet. "Anything interesting happen since you've been gone?"

"Well," he replied, "not too much. I've been gone not even a month now. But one of my neighbor's sons got married this last weekend. My neighbor said it was quite nice. The days were no longer so hot, so they could have a ceremony in the late afternoon, and when it got colder at night, they had a few people play guitars around a fire."

"Well, that sounds quite nice, eh?" She spoke with a pleasant smile.

His eyes were distant, and he nodded his head lightly. "Yes."

A few moments went by, and the train clicked and clacked as usual.

"You seem somewhat distraught," she said, the afternoon sun dancing on her face.

"Oh? Well, you know," explained Cezal casually. "It's the same story everywhere—others living their lives, growing up, moving on, getting married, starting families, the standard spiel."

"And you feel like you're behind?" she said, not taking her eyes off the crochet.

"Well, I suppose that's one way to put it. It's not just that I feel behind, but it's actually the kind of life I would like—settling down and having a family and the stability and all. I'm a rather simple person. I don't need much excitement. But, I'm getting older now, and I wonder if I'll ever have that life.

I try to be okay with it, but you know, there's a certain sense of loss that comes and goes."

She nodded. "What's to say you won't have it? By most standards, really, you've still got quite a lot ahead of you. And I know you're looking forward to the mundane, but I feel like it's important to tell you that you can look at life as being so front-loaded with all the exciting things happening when you're young, and all the boring, stable things as being part of your monotonous, bran-filled future." She paused to shrug her shoulders. "But it doesn't have to be that way. So if you feel like you've missed out, that's up to you as to whether it stays that way."

Cezal looked into his cup at the barley sediment that began to collect at the bottom.

"Well… I suppose there's some truth in that," Cezal replied, feeling she had missed his point somewhat. "I suppose I feel like I've missed many of the normal milestones of development that lead up to living that kind of life. I don't know," he trailed off. "I don't want to sound hyperbolic, but you begin to feel as though there's something most other people understand, and they're all connected by a sort of fabric of society that makes them all human. I try to get into that fabric, but whenever I try to, it's like batting at a curtain. You begin to wonder what you don't get. And so I see your point that it's up to me to make my life, but I think it's not through laziness or self-pity that I feel like I'm behind, but more so I just don't know how to get there."

A baby somewhere a few cabins down started to cry. It stopped a few moments later, presumably after being fed.

"Perhaps this will come off as insensitive, but to be honest, Cezal, I don't have a real answer for you. All I can say is not to think on it too much, though I know that's hardly any consolation. In the end, though, all you can do is try to be the best person you can be. If you keep good and pure intentions, I think if you stumble around enough, you'll eventually find a way into the fabric. And really, venturing out of that small town you've lived in your entire life is, I would think, a rather big step in the right direction. That said, though, don't forget the value of the other things in life. If you put all your hopes on getting into the proverbial fabric, you'll realize you've wasted too much time trying to get into something that likely doesn't really exist in the way you think it does. It's like we talked about before—your life has started, don't make the mistake of waiting all night for the show to begin."

He nodded, and she stared out the window for a bit. Cezal looked back at her, at her deeply wrinkled face and crochet resting calmly in her lap. It was almost comical how grand-motherly she seemed. He looked back out the window, and she looked back at Cezal, with his comfortable and border-line dirty summer clothes—the brown linen shirt unbut-toned three buttons, paired with the faded canvas pants.

She looked back at him. "You're also not the only one who feels the way you do. We live in an age of emptiness, you know. That's why there are so many ideologues going around trying to start this movement, or that political party, or take over this city. It's all a game they play. More and more people nowadays, like you, are looking for something more, and the ideologues claim to have a solution. I wonder if perhaps this time will come to be remembered by that quiet dissatisfaction most people live with."

"Quiet dissatisfaction?" Cezal asked.

She raised her eyebrows. "Don't tell me you've already forgotten? You don't consider yourself dissatisfied?"

"With what?" he asked.

"Well, from what you've said, with life," she replied.

He stared at her for a moment.

"Oh, I suppose so," he said.

"Well, at the very least, I don't think you're alone. And as I've said before, we've forgotten the importance of community, and having a family or a job of high stature isn't the only way to find meaningfulness in your life. It's because we've become so collectively isolated that we've come to view having a family almost as a means of escape, which is what it sounds like you do." She picked up her crochet and began again. "As I said before, people have a hard time facing themselves. But that's a big part of why I sit here on this train, why I enjoy talking to people, getting to share some of my story. It's important, too, that we engage other people with our whole personality—delve beneath the surface. That is how people develop themselves and have meaningful interactions. Don't waste your time with superficial people. After all, conversations about the weather never helped anyone. And besides, it's a nice comfort, really, just to talk as we do. I do thank you for that, Cezal." She looked at him with kind eyes. "Sometimes as well, it's important to remind oneself to appreciate simply sharing company with one another."

And so, with the clack of the train and the trees sauntering past, they sat for some time in silence just like that, enjoying each other's company.

* * *

The next morning, after Cezal secured some hard-boiled eggs and rye bread with sunflower seeds from one of the side vendors at the last stop, he took breakfast with Iljantva. It was quite picturesque, like the romantic sort of breakfast one imagines passengers of the trains of antiquity as having had. By this point, they had gotten to a grand mountain range. It was certainly not as stunning as the Dolomites and nor as fabled as the Atlas mountains. Still, they were beautiful nonetheless, with the sun glistening down through the wide, blue sky, onto the tall green grasses and fields of red, yellow, and orange wildflowers. Summer in the north—there's nothing quite like it.

For some time, the train was between the mountain face on one end and a wonderful lake on the other. And quite the lake it was. It was nearly an hour they were simply going along it, with the track curving every so often to better hug the mountain, bringing into view different angles of the landscape. The train had to go much slower here because of all the curves, but the picturesque quality of the world was lost on no one.

Accordingly, Iljantva and Cezal ate in relative silence, taking in the landscape instead.

After some time of this, Cezal broke in. "You know, Iljantva, you've talked quite a bit, but I don't really know much about you."

"No?" she asked.

"Well, not really. For example, I don't know much about where you're going or why you're going there."

"Ah," she laughed lightly. "Well, I supposed I never really talked about it in detail because there's not much to be said."

"Sure there is. I'd be interested in hearing what you have to say," he replied.

She paused a moment and wiped her mouth before leaning back a bit.

"Well… I suppose I've always been somewhat of a romantic, dreaming of faraway, exotic places and picturesque views. It's nice to have things to romanticize. But yes, ever since I was a little girl, I've dreamt of going to somewhere different from where I grew up. I, like you, lived in the same area my whole life, but I knew many stories from other lands and always had a sense of wonder for them. But, yes, I was a florist, and so I stayed in place most of my life. And by no means was it a bad life, but it certainly didn't afford one much time for travel." She looked out the window with a smile. "And I took care of my neighbors as they took care of me. And I knew my little town well, and it knew me well. Almost everyone came around my shop at some point or another, even if just the local kids looking to laze about and get respite from the summer heat. Yes, it was nice those days." She looked wistfully into the distance with a light smile and soft eyes. She looked back at Cezal after some time. "But, after a while, I realized I'm not getting younger as you can see, so it seemed rather the time for an adventure." And she gave a kind smile. "As I said before, the village I'm going to is known for their flowers and have a spring flower festival. Perhaps I'll stick around long enough to get to see it. Quite nice, the village is. I've seen photos before."

She looked at Cezal and then back out the window. "Fall is coming soon, I suppose, eh Cezal?"

"I suppose it is, isn't it?" He watched her face and the way she moved her mouth as she stared out the window, as though wanting to say something, and perhaps even having a conversation in her head, but without vocalizing anything.

"Sometimes, my dear," she finally said, "all you can do is appreciate that you're alive and give yourself a wry smile. There are many of us who, as we age, have only our memories to comfort us. I'm lucky in that I have quite good ones."

* * *

They had exited the mountain range during the night, so when the morning sun began to filter through the sheer curtains, the landscape was far flatter, though still filled with trees: mostly pine and aspen. There were now more frequently streams and larger rivers through which the train wound its way. And while the inside of the train was nearly always overheated, leading one to try and leave the windows open, by now, in the early morning, everything was at a rather comfortable temperature, if not even a bit cold, resulting in Cezal's getting up to close the window before leaving to get their breakfast tea.

Upon returning, he found Iljantva had bought them both some rye bread and jam. As they sat down to eat, he asked her to tell him more about the ideologues she had mentioned before. They weren't so common an occurrence where Cezal was from.

She looked up from her bread and tea and nodded. "Well, to frame it in a more disinterested way, I suppose they can be described as people who see the vacuousness of our times and the loneliness people feel and essentially try to fix it. Of course, though, most of them aren't doing it out of a deep love of humanity, but rather out of an opportunistic thirst for power. Their popularity waxes and wanes as time goes on. I think they're most popular in the small cities in the East. That's where people seem to feel the most trapped by their lives." She took a bite of toast. "I make it a point to avoid such people—ideologues, that is. Once the novelty of meeting such a sort of person runs out, there's little value they have." She paused a second and took a bite of bread. "Well, I shouldn't talk of them so disparagingly. They are usually very charismatic. I've heard people even describe them as addicting to be around, and from my experience, that doesn't sound like too much of an exaggeration. But they make, really, for rather poor friends."

"Why is that?" Cezal asked.

She shook her head a bit and shrugged her shoulders. "Well… I suppose it's because they want power, and their job is to figure out how to get it. And that's best done by manipulating people and making them think they'll solve whatever problems you have with the world. The vast majority of them do nothing more than sell snake oil intended to mend the human spirit. Of course, though, just as snake oil is nothing but mineral water and turpentine, the salvation provided by ideologues is most always nothing but cheap lies and nice-sounding stories told to hide uncomfortable truths. They'll make you believe in yourself again—make you think you're something special, but once you no longer serve a purpose for them, you'll be thrown away without a second thought."

"I see," replied Cezal. The train continued to clack in the chilled air as the trees sauntered by.

"Yes," she continued. "But I suppose it's a job that will always exist in one way or another. I would condemn them, but I think in some cases, they do help."

"You think so?" Cezal asked, raising his eyebrows in an assuming way.

She shrugged her shoulders and tilted her head slightly to the side. "I'd say so. They lie and manipulate, but sometimes that's what people need. Everyone is fragile in some way or another, and there will come a time in everyone's life where they'll feel like a child who's scared and hurt. Who needs someone big and strong to kiss their little scrape. Someone to wrap their arms around when there's a thunderstorm, and it's dark out. Someone who, even when you hate yourself the most, will give you a caring and understanding hug and who will whisper, 'It'll be all right' as they hold you in their arms." She took another bite of bread, leaning her head down as she swallowed and following it with a sip of tea to wash it down. "People, my dear, are little children at heart. We all want to be loved and wanted and cherished. We want to know we matter to others, and they're glad we're here. That's the best gift you can give someone. That's all really we can ever give. To tell someone else you love them for everything they are and everything they're not. Don't underestimate that. For some, I think you'll find, love isn't enough, and that's a difficult thing to accept when faced with it." She paused a moment and looked out the window at the passing greenery. "But I digress. Ideologues give something like love and acceptance. At least, they make someone feel loved in a certain way. It's not authentic, no, but not everyone is looking for authenticity. If you can't be truly loved and made to feel cherished by someone else, then at least an ideologue can pretend to care about you. And for many really, that's enough to get by."

They looked at each other for a few moments. "That sounds rather dark, I must say. Do you really think so many people are doomed to live in such a way?"

"Of course not," she balked. "No one is ever doomed to anything. I'm speaking simply to what often happens—not what should or can. There is a value to truly reconning with yourself—a value in picking yourself up off the floor a countless number of times. But most people won't. I would certainly suggest one not settle for the comfort found in an ideologue. But nor can I deny the utility they provide. For you, Cezal, I would warn you against it. You seem rather weak-willed at first, but I think you know yourself well enough not to need to settle for someone like that." Again, she fell silent for some time, but

Cezal could see her thinking. She sighed. "There will come a time in your life when you realize there is no one to reckon with but yourself. You will see a path before you, be that the path of bitterness or love, self-pity or resilience, of love or hate, or of fleeting fulfillment or dissatisfaction. It will be up to you then to ask yourself which you want. There is no justice in the world, and most likely, you will be faced with these decisions when you feel that lack of justice sting you the most. But you do not forgive for the sake of the other; you do not pick yourself off from the floor for the sake of the other; you do not love yourself for the sake of the other. You do it for yourself. It is then when you will understand how forgiveness frees."

She took another sip and Cezal remembered his tea, and drank some too. "And while my mentioning of forgiveness may seem tangential, I say it because people become bitter when they see they are truly alone or the ideologue who once showered them with roses is now nowhere to be found. Bitterness and disappointment—those are some of the most caustic effects of an ideologue. And so, Cezal, you must love yourself because you cannot expect anyone else to. We are alone, my dear, very alone. Nothing can change that, I'm afraid. I've seen that realization consume people. They become sickly beings burdened by the weight of existence, by the paradox of it all. The world for them is a vast graveyard of lost dreams and disillusionment. They become melancholy and morose. They fade away. Away into existence." She looked into the distance as though watching a balloon slowly rise into the sky. "It's a sad thing to see, and many people will fall down that path. My dear, you can't listen to the chitter-chatter, you'll just grow weary and bitter far before your time. There's nothing to do but to get up again and again and struggle. Smile through it all, my dear, or cry if that feels right. There are a precious few things that really matter in life, so take the important stuff seriously and try to remind yourself that everything else doesn't matter that much."

Cezal nodded. "That's good advice."

Iljantva nodded in turn. "I hope you don't find it too forward. I get the feeling you're going to be disappointed when you finally get to Briedavga—once the novelty of it wears off. That's why I tell you these things."

He nodded again and looked down at his nearly finished bread. "Perhaps you're right. I'll look out for it."

* * *

Mildew, that particular smell, filled the room as Alja awoke. It was dark—the time between day and night, when even the twilight hour was over, and a deep blue filled the world and flowed into the room, over her. Nothing in the room had much color, such was the lack of light. The cabin was empty and silent, and she listened to her breath, the calm inhale and exhale, and watched the room grow darker.

There were many wooden containers of various sizes laying about the entire room, none larger in proportion than the length of her foot. She walked among them, on the gently creaking floor, for some time, pondering their particular shape and texture: the dovetailing and the sanding. *They're just boxes*, she thought and continued to pace around the darkening room, the damp stillness filling her.

But then, it was time to get to work.

She sat on the floor, her legs folded beneath her, and carefully, she slid in the half-darkness the first box over. She looked inside and saw someone's memory—two children playing in a field of fall leaves. After a while, she slid the lid back on and put it to the side and looked into another. The next box contained the memory of a book she had read as a child. She looked into another one and saw a memory of suffering and coldness. She tried to reach in, but it was only a moving picture, nothing more. She closed it. The other boxes were more of the same—memories and experiences and dreams of other times and places. She looked into them, and in turn, they looked into her. She saw everything she was and everything she could ever be contained in them—in all the sundry details and unique facets. It was enjoyable, looking into them, these windows to another world.

She tried to look into the first box again—the one with the children playing in the leaves but found it was gone. There was a different memory in its stead: a woman talking to a man.

Eventually, after a long time, she felt emptier and so stopped looking.

She walked around the room once more, quietly pacing, her feet making the soft sound that feet make when walking barefoot on a hardwood floor, the creaking sounding like someone else's this time around.

It was nearly completely dark. One could only see black and a deep blue in the place where the windows were. The silence once again washed over her.

She knew where the vanity mirror was and walked over to it.

She stared into the dark, and it stared back.

"Is that you, Alja?" her reflection asked.

"Yes," she replied.

"No, it is not," it said.

"Why not?" she asked.

"Because you only pretend to be her."

"Oh," she replied. "Of course, how could I have forgotten."

And by then, it was fully night, and there was no light left.

* * *

It had been raining rather heavily. The muffled pitter-patter of the drops blanketed themselves on the roof of the train. Someone from the family in the cabin next to Cezal and Iljantva's forgot to close their window. Early in the morning, when it was no longer rainy, and instead the sky was filled with full, billowy clouds, Cezal sat with his tea watching the sun rise over the rolling hills.

A skirmish broke out next door over the absentminded fellow who forgot to close the window.

"Eh, wake up! Molit! Wake up!

"Eah… what…"

Cezal could imagine him, probably wearing a white tank top and underwear, rolling over—still half asleep, just barely lifting his face out of a likely drool-soaked pillow.

"Look at this—it's all wet! I told you! I told you, Molit, once you got back last night, close the window! That's not too complicated for you, is it?"

"Ehh, no need to be mean."

"Mean? Do a simple task and then tell me not to be mean!"

"Shh, you'll wake the kids. All right, I forgot to close the window. It's not the end of the world. Let me wake up a second, and then I'll go get some pins for the clothesline."

The train entered a tunnel, so alas, Cezal was no longer privy to the drama unfolding next door. A few minutes later, a short, scruffy man wearing an oversized, buttoned shirt and presumably underwear, shuffled past Cezal's door in slippers. One could only assume to get pins.

A moment later, Iljantva turned over, still in bed, and yawned.

"Quite the lively way to start the morning, eh Cezal."

"Yes, lively indeed." He smiled and nodded his head. "Would you like me to get you some tea?"

"Oh yes, that would be wonderful, my dear. I still need to get some packing done." She sat up and shuffled around some papers on her side table until she found her itinerary.

"Yes, we stop at Zebbere a bit before noon."

"Ah, so you can take your time then."

"Yes, it's not horribly strenuous."

They had a pleasant teatime and made idle chatter as one does in such situations, then after a while, the conversation slowed down, and they took to looking out at the window at the scenery. Now still, there were more often clearings in the trees, more rolling hills, and even more streams. There too, were increasingly frequent signs of human settlement. They passed some stone bridges (and the odd farmer with a fishing rod, sitting stoically), a few houses with smoke coming out of the chimney, and fields for this or that crop. The train had begun to head in a more southerly direction after the mountain range, and so the sun was shining here more intensely— one could feel it warming their skin, glimmering wonderfully.

"You live alone, don't you, Iljantva?"

She looked at him and adjusted herself.

"Well, yes, it's been like that for a while now."

"Do you ever feel rather lonely?" he asked.

She thought for a moment.

"Yes, I do. You know, I never married or had kids. For a while, that bothered me quite a bit because I felt like I was running out of time. I think similarly to you, I felt like I was missing developmental milestones. Yes, it used to quite bother me. Sometimes it would particularly get to me, and I'd cry myself to sleep, aching to hold someone in my arms." She gave a wry smile and shifted how she sat. "But that was long ago now. For some time, I lamented what there was to lament, but after a while, I realized this sadness I felt for what could have been was exactly that. I was sad about what *could* have been, but never was. It was as though I thought if I marinated long enough in what I wished would have been, I would start to get that in reality—that I would become less lonely. But of course, that wasn't the case. I eventually woke up one day and realized I was missing something that never was, that never would be. It was not some alternate reality I was missing. There is no what could have been; there is simply what was. And what was is that I never had children or a husband. Of course, though, I had my friends and my community and my own hobbies and interests and work. Because of that, I wasn't alone in any sense of the word."

Cezal nodded. "Do you regret it? Do you feel like you missed out?"

She shook her head and closed a bag that was next to her. "I don't regret it, no. Though I was the kind of person who really did want to have that kind of familial life—or at least I think I would have. Of course, now I don't really know. Perhaps I did miss out on some things. But it doesn't matter—had I had that familial life, I would have missed out on other things my actual life I've led has provided me. And that's why I told you not to worry about ending up an old grape like me. I don't lament my choices or regret my life. There's still quite a lot to get up each day for."

Cezal continued to look at her, some disappointment in his eyes.

"So you think I really am behind?" he asked.

"Perhaps so," she replied. "But I didn't tell you this before because I didn't want you to worry about it. Maybe you'll catch up, and maybe not. Either way, though, you'll be okay."

She smiled a bit. "As you get older, you get your priorities better in line, and you realize that really, it's all okay—it's almost always okay."

He smiled a bit and took a breath. "That's a bit difficult to accept."

"Perhaps so, but you just may have to."

They sat in silence for some time, listening to the muffled chitter-chatter of the other cabins, the sun streaming in just a vibrantly as ever. After some time, Iljantva spoke again.

"'You'll find what you look for in life.' That's what my aunt used to tell me. And she was right. Yes, you may end up dying single, but that doesn't mean you have to die filled with regret. If you look for love and beauty, you will find it. You will find it because in doing so, you will realize it is something that has always existed in you. Those who look for happiness or love outside of themselves will always be dissatisfied. It is like decorating your house with paintings and expecting to become a skilled painter yourself. To make a beautiful painting, you must paint. Similarly, to fill your life with love, you yourself must first love. You cannot rely upon other people and expect them to complete you. It is something one must cultivate in oneself."

And the scenery continued to go by, with the summer sun, the flowers, the rolling hills, and the increasing number of people working the fields. Iljantva and Cezal sat there, taking it all in.

* * *

At last, the conductor came by to announce they would soon be in Zebbere. By this time, there was no longer a forest but rather rolling hills covered with wildflowers of red, yellow, purple, blue, and white, with the grasses growing in a lovely shade of green, all basking in the immaculate sunlight. As they got closer, the fields were all filled with yellow flowers—used to make Canola oil, Iljantva told him. Soon, more and more houses and roads went by, with children and adults alike walking about on the beautiful day. The clouds were high and wispy in the sky, complementing the resplendent blue that surrounded them.

"Well, here we are," Cezal said.

"Here we are," Iljantva repeated, nodding. Cezal got up to get her green-leathered suitcase out of the top storage area. In addition to her suitcase, she had a little knit bag she put on her back. Cezal slid open the door, and they stepped out into the corridor and walked to the exit. Cezal stepped off the train with Iljantva. It was humid there, and on the platform, the heat was almost oppressive, but with all the people coming and going, it felt lively and chatter filled.

"Well, this is it," Cezal stated. "Thank you for your advice."

Iljantva gave him a twinkly-eyed smile. "Well, thank you for listening to me. It's been nice. Good luck in Briedavga."

The train conductor blew his whistle, and people began to disperse.

"Well, I suppose I should get back on the train," Cezal said.

Iljantva smiled. "Yes, I suppose you should. Goodbye now. I wish you all the best. Be kind to yourself."

"Yes, I will be," Cezal replied. "And the same to you."

He walked back onto the train and sat down at his old seat in the cabin and stared out the window at the platform. Iljantva was already making her way to the train terminal. Endings were sad, he supposed. And he marinated for a little while in the goodbye as he looked at the warm, summer day and thought of all the lives of the people on the platform, all with their immense complexities and all with their hopes and dreams and struggles he'd never know about. And at that moment, there was a certain beauty to the world that hit him, and so he steeped in that beautiful, melancholic wonder until the train whistle sounded again, this time thrice, as the train groaned to a start in the sluggish way they always do.

He continued to stare out the window for quite some time, watching as the train gathered speed and went through the town, with its many people and yellow flower fields and stone bridges and playing children. Then, it was the forest again, and there were only pine trees in the afternoon sun.

5

———

It was nice for Cezal to have the cabin to himself for a while. He slowly spread his belongings out to fill the entire space, with a book here or there, his clothes laid out on both beds, some crackers on the fold-out table, along with a notebook and some letters. His reprieve, however, lasted only until the following afternoon, when Cezal noticed a tall figure standing in the doorway—a young man in clothes that at one point probably would have been considered dapper enough to go about town, but that now, after a few years and likely more than a few wearers, were rather worn. Though compared to the rather haggard lot that was most other passengers, this character wore his velvet corduroy pants and similarly colored jacket with a unique vitality. Underneath, he had a white, moderately sweat-stained, Egyptian cotton, button-up shirt, and a diagonally striped tie of that same maroon with navy and light blue to complement it. This all was topped off by brown leather shoes and white socks. How he wasn't suffering heatstroke by this point was beyond Cezal, though some people, it would seem, are simply meant for the heat.

"Hello, I believe this is the cabin for my reservation. I'm Zamen." He stretched out his arm to Cezal's, who seemed to be rather caught off guard, as evidenced by his absentmind-edly shaking Zamen's hand before getting up and clearing the bed, apologizing lightly for the mess.

"No need to rush. Here, let me help you," Zamen said, pro-ceeding to help him fold the clothes off the bed while making some clever and disarming remark about them, probably comparing them to his own somewhat shabby attire.

The following days continued without much exchange. He asked Cezal to pass him the salt once during a meal. Out of boredom, Cezal occasionally tried to make conversation with him.

"What's that you're reading?"

"Where are you headed to?"

"I'm getting a cup of tea. Would you like one?"

Zamen was pleasant enough, though his responses reflected only the minimum requirement for social pleasantry.

"Oh, it's just a book a friend gave to me before I left."

"I'm headed pretty far east to a small town—almost no one's heard of it, but I have some work to do there."

"No, thank you, I've already had some."

And so Cezal left it at that and simply took to observing him from time to time between reading his own books, or writing, or staring out the window.

It seemed to him Zamen was always reading something or another—a book, or a newspaper, or even the almanac of the town Cezal assumed he was heading to. He noted his habit of writing in short spurts on the margins of the newspapers and gazettes, annotating some article or another. Afterward, Zamen would open his notebook and look over the annotations and flip through some pages or write some-thing new down there. Every so often, he would write to have a telegram sent out.

Cezal must have been watching him for a week or so before his curiosity finally got the best of him.

"Perhaps I'm being a bit forward, Zamen, but you seem rather an interesting figure. If you have the time and desire, I'd enjoy having a more substantive conversation with you."

Zamen looked up from his newspaper, his legs folded, the paper atop them, held on both sides by his commanding hands.

He gave a bemused smile. "What would you like to know?"

"Well," replied Cezal, "I suppose I'm curious where you're going and why you're going there."

"Ah, you're quite a forward one, aren't you?" he replied with a cheeky smile.

Cezal looked at him somewhat taken aback and started a half-stuttered response.

"Please take no offense," Zamen interjected. "I meant nothing by it. I simply say what's on my mind. I'm headed to a small town in the east, as I've said before. It's called Kevelga, and I plan to try to make a name for myself there. I don't know where you're from, but perhaps you've heard of my line of work. I'm an 'ideologue,' as they say. They're becoming more and more common around these parts. That's part of the reason I have to go so far east to make something of myself." He stopped a moment before adding casually, "Ah, but either way, the more removed and backwater a place is, the better I'll be able to work."

By then, Cezal had been leaning forward, a look of intrigue on his face. "Yes, I have heard of ideologues before, though I must admit, I've never met one in person. What is it exactly that you all do?"

Zamen took a breath and shrugged his shoulders a bit, uncrossing his legs and leaning in, putting the paper to his side. "Well, at its most simple, really, I suppose what we do is try to create and consolidate power." He paused to take a sip of tea. "If you've heard of us, I assume you know we're rather controversial figures. I speak so frankly with you only because you don't seem like the kind of person to have been steeping in the vitriol long enough to develop an automatic, and in my opinion unwarranted, disdain for what we do. But yes, the more charitable description of an ideologue is someone who is a fixer, so to speak. We're someone who goes into any group of people or a city or a country even and is able to perceive and understand the different dynamics that are at play. We can see through all the ego and the suffering and anger to be able to help build a better society—a sort of cross between a sage and a politician."

Cezal smiled and nodded. "I see. And the less charitable description?"

Zamen gave a light laugh. "Ah yes. Well, those who don't like us would consider us egotistical, even evil, brutes who have no real skills, so we restructure society to make it work for us."

Cezal stared at him a second. "And what do you think?"

"Well…" began Zamen, waving his arms up playfully. "What *I* think is largely irrelevant, but there's some truth to both sides. I'd like to think, though, that my heart is in the right place."

Cezal leaned back, not sure what to make of this character before him.

"Oh, I know there's a certain level of sliminess to what we do. I get it. It's not exactly the most honorable line of work; that is, unless you're successful. But believe me, I get it. It seems like we're just here to manipulate people, but there is true, good intention behind it. You know, back in my hometown, my father was a cobbler, making many a shoe. And you know, it's good business. People need shoes," he said, gently throwing both of his forearms up with palms open while shrugging his shoulders. "Ah, but it was never the life for me. I find stability stifling, at least at this point in time. So I left town and sold what I had to get a few more years of education. And besides, I have a couple of younger siblings, so my parents weren't too worried about the family business going by the wayside. So now I'm here. In search of a new life."

Cezal leaned back again, looking at the bright-eyed man before him, and gave a wistful sigh. "Well, that's quite the story."

By then, it was late afternoon, and the late summer sun cast its particular, gentle gaze onto the trees as they continued east. The conversation continued, and Cezal explained why he himself was on the train. They talked somewhat late into the night until Zamen said he needed to get more reading in, and Cezal, in turn, went to sleep.

* * *

Chummy. That is how Cezal and Zamen seemed after a few days of talking together. They took to drinking many nights, most often to a far greater extent than Cezal ever had with Iljantva. Not infrequently, they would come to adopt a level of borderline raucous behavior and conviviality that would draw the ire of the early risers and the companionship of the more free-spirited. Their cramped parties often lasted into the late hours of the night and were punctuated with good storytelling, much-spirited debate, and deep conversation, entertaining even the less inclined of the drinkers—virtue of the loose-lippedness that invariably accompanied such discussions.

On one such night many hours after the drinking began, with wine and vodka bottles strewn around their small cabin, Zamen waved his arm dismissively at Cezal and another passenger, a haggard grandpa in a white tank top. An energetic "bah!" issued from Zamen's mouth. "It's about the dream—the *dream*, Cezal. Don't you see it?"

Cezal stared back with a drunken vacantness that seemed to be occupying his face increasingly often.

"Ah, you'll see it at some point, I'm sure," Zamen conceded. "There's a certain inescapable futility to it all—everything I'm doing. Yes, I'm planning my revolution or whatever you wish to call it, but ah, how likely will I be successful? Probably not likely. But I'm alive. I'm *alive*, and that's a fact that's more valuable than most people realize."

The train clacked through the darkness. At the head of Cezal's bed, next to the scruffy grandpa, was a passed out businessman-type figure drooling into the covers, his body awkwardly lain on the mattress—feet on the floor and torso sprawled across the sheets behind Cezal and the grandpa.

"Ah, but that's the point of it really. It's about the dream," continued Zamen. "It's about the attempt. Look at all this around us, look at these people." Cezal and the grandpa looked around at the passed out fellow next to them, and the two drunkenly entranced faces on Zamen's bed, looking at him as though the purveyor of Truth. "Look at what we're doing, look at who we are. We're nothing—we're nothing. But none of it is important. It's all that we have. It's all that's real in this moment.

"Yes, we sit here and steep in our conviviality. What else is there to do, eah? And that's the thing," Zamen emphasized. "So little of what we do is important. You come to realize how inconsequential everything really is. And you accept that fact after a while, and you look around at the world, and you see how it's all a game. It's all a game." He shrugged his shoulders energetically. "What is there to do but embrace it? That's why I'm in it—this game. I'm going to Kevelga. I'm gonna try and start my revolution that's full of shit, and everybody will know it. But I'm gonna do it."

He paused for dramatic effect. Though in the group's drunken stupor, it didn't feel overdone.

He pointed his finger at no one in particular. "And I'm going to make sure I succeed. But I know it's nothing. And you all know it's nothing." Zamen looked around at everyone. "But the people will follow. And I'll be forever indebted to them for it. Because that's what it all is, that's all we really are—people to be manipulated. We all want to follow someone. I'm sure you know Dostoyevsky. You know people don't actually want freedom. And I know well enough just how unimportant everything is to want power. So I'll get it. I'll lead the people. I'll get done what needs to be done."

They continued to stare. One man asked Cezal to pass the wine.

"Will the people be satisfied, though?" Zamen continued to muse. "Will I live up to their expectations? Of course not. It will never be that. It can never be that. The world, as you all already know, is a disappointment. But it's up to you to be disappointed by that fact or not. And so I expect nothing of it," he shrugged. "I expect the people to hate me, and I expect to hate them for it. Ah, but in this way, you see the futility of it all. How can one not help but embrace that with one's whole being, eh? It's really quite special."

Zamen asked the man next to him to pass the wine back, took a few swigs, and placed the empty bottle on the table.

"There's a part of me that does hate myself," Zamen continued, this time more quietly, more pensively, "There is. There is. But I know on a deeper level it doesn't matter. I don't matter enough to *truly* hate, and no one matters enough to truly hate. And so my paltry revolution will be just that. And I'll fade into the annals of history and will be forgotten by all but those who themselves lived through it. But how can I complain? I'll have my moment in the sun. I'll make of it what I can. My dream. My life-affirming dream." And he looked in the direction of the ceiling, both his palms faceup, outstretched. "And so that's what I live for. It won't be successful. I know almost certainly because how many people succeed? I think I have a chance—I do. But on a more conscious level, I know I probably won't. And you know, to be honest with you, I think I'm evil. I think I am. But that's okay." He leaned back a bit and chuckled to himself.

One of the men on his side of the bed tried to chime in. "Oh, don't tell yourself that, Zamen."

Zamen nodded his head emphatically. "No, no, thank you, but it's okay," he replied. "I don't need to be good. Because like I said before: it doesn't really matter. *I* don't really matter."

Zamen noticed the ragged grandpa raised his eyebrows disapprovingly. "Ah, look at you taken aback," said Zamen. "Bah, don't listen to me. I'm just rambling on like any old drunk you'd find. Don't take me too seriously."

The mustachioed grandpa just grumped to himself and took another swig from his flask.

"But," Zamen began again, "it's interesting to think about what my life really is—what your life really is, or what anyone's is for that matter. What are we doing? We're sitting around on a train getting drunk. And for what? I mean, hah, why not, I suppose. You know, I guess what more could one ask for? But yes, I have a dream. A dreadful dream, but a dream, nonetheless. I plan to start a revolution, and I plan to be successful." At that, Zamen dramatically turned to stare directly at Cezal. "Tell me, Cezal, do you plan to be successful?"

The previously passed out businessman broke in before Cezal could respond. "Oh come now, you old coot, you've gone on long enough. Just let us get some rest." That spurred the two people sitting next to Zamen to glance at their wristwatches and begin to make their excuses. The night wound down from there.

* * *

The cold light of morning. That was the expression that came to Cezal's mind after waking up with barely any sleep. He sluggishly sat up in bed, ears ringing, and eyes pierced by the sun. He pulled the drapes over the windows and went out to get a cup of breakfast tea for Zamen and himself. Zamen was still asleep on the other side of the cabin, so Cezal set the cups on the table and stared at the opposing wall, giving particular attention to faux-wood paneling. He felt it in the air: summer was ending. It was a feeling unlike any other and couldn't be missed even in the train's stuffy cabins.

He was the type to ruminate on the past, so he mulled over his and Zamen's various conversations and milquetoast misadventures. It was a semi pleasant experience—almost cathartic with his tea and the clacking of the train.

After a little while, Zamen, too, sat up, looking less haggard than one would expect. He scooched over to the table and thanked Cezal for the now lukewarm tea.

"I take it you'd prefer to keep the drapes drawn?" Zamen asked.

"You can open the one on your side. I'll adjust," Cezal replied.

He nodded and stirred some sugar into his tea.

"I've been thinking more about what you said last night about what you're really trying to do," Cezal said.

"Mm," Zamen replied, still looking out the window. "What about it?"

Cezal shrugged his shoulders, "It's interesting. Most people aren't like that. Don't think I'm trying to compliment you," he added playfully. "You seem to have a big enough ego already. But regardless, it's something one takes note of. It's not as though most get the idea to try to start a revolution, or whatever it is you're going to do. What exactly is your plan, though?"

Zamen looked away from the window to address Cezal. "Well, that's a good question," he chuckled. "I really won't know until I get there. I'll do my best to understand how the different power dynamics play out—who's in charge, which the powerful families are, what makes them tick, what's not working right, etc. You know, that kind of thing. I chose this town because there's a fair degree of turmoil at this time. That's why I'm always reading newspapers and historical books. I'm trying to keep up with the town's goings-on and understand its history. If I have it figured out correctly, I should be able to do some odd jobs here and there, hear from people what they like and dislike, what they wish the rulers did differently, that kind of thing. Then, after a few months, I'll have made enough connections to understand the people well enough and for them to feel comfortable with me. Then, I'll go to the main city square, get up on a soapbox—most likely literally—and I'll give them an impassioned speech that, if successful, will make them believe in the future again."

"I see," Cezal said, not quite sure of what to make of the plan. He felt no need to try and get him to do more sensible things. "And why did you want to do this in the first place?"

Zamen looked at him, then down, into his nearly finished tea, and readjusted himself on the bed so he could better lean forward before looking back at Cezal. "Well, in my youth, I was always a rather timid type. I followed the rules and planned to be a cobbler—follow in my father's footsteps. Ah, but I always looked at the profession with a certain inevitability: There was no real desire I had for it. Others told me that's just how it is and to be happy. I have a good future lined up. And they were right, but I realized I don't live for them, and nor do I live for a joyless future. After that realization, I came to be increasingly fed up listening to the advice and narratives of others. I found them vapid and unimpressive. And mind you," he said, raising his forearm off the table in an explanatory way, "it wasn't just their life path I found unimpressive, but their conception of self—the way they looked at the world. Most of them seemed to me far too self-satisfied for their own good. And so, perhaps half out of boredom and half out of resentment, once I felt I understood someone's conception of self well enough, I started to make my own narratives of them and, with enough time and deftness, I saw I was able to make them start to adopt my own narrative of who they were."

Cezal raised his eyebrows. "How do you mean?"

He shrugged. "Oh, well, it just takes some time and understanding. Make them feel safe and understood around you. Then you can see better what motivates them. Those with a big ego, for example, but who were oblivious to it, were the easiest to manipulate. Make them think you look up to them and help them build themself up and you're quite well-liked. Once they've let you in, it becomes easier to bring things to their attention or spin the interpretation of events in a certain way."

"Can you give an example?" Cezal interjected.

"Well," Zamen hemmed, "each person is different. I think it would qualify as an art, really. There are no concrete rules. You just have to practice it. But anyhow, being able to change people's narratives of themself and their world: that is the root of ideology. And when you get down to it, most people are emptier than you would think. They cling to grand narratives, to their nationality, to their religion, to their place in society, to the clothes they wear. Without these things, most people are empty." He leaned back a bit and crossed his legs. "But eah, all the easier to fill them up with whatever you want. And really, it's in this vacuum that the ideologue thrives. You see, there is always the potential for power. Why you ask?" he said, smiling a bit at Cezal. "Well, perhaps this sounds rather cheesy coming from me, but the reason is that, for someone who is power hungry, other people inherently have power and value. It's the narcissist who arguably needs other people the most. Most of the time, people don't realize they're so necessary. They are prey, really. The ideologue is thus a magician, if I may so dramatize my tentative profession, channeling the power of many people into a single person, institution, or ideology. Just as the magician conducts their magic through a wand, the ideologue conducts their magic through ideology."

"Mm, go on," Cezal replied, taking a sip of tea.

"Well, think back to the people last night. Most of them looked rather weathered, myself included. I think it's safe to say they aren't happy. I, too, was like this. I was on the path to becoming just like the grandpa from last night. I'll bet our little drinking soirée will be the highlight of his whole trip. But I digress. Like I said before, I got fed up after a while with my life as it was. I asked myself where it got me, and I wasn't satisfied with my answer. So I decided to make it different."

At this point, Zamen was getting more and more into his monologue and began to motion with his arms to dramatize his speech, as though giving an impassioned sermon.

"I looked at the desert around me, Cezal, and was tired of thirsting, tired of overheating. And so, I resolved to make my world an oasis. Now that I'm an ideologue, my oasis will quench not only my thirst but the thirst of all the gasping people in the desert of meaning. Of course, I have no final solution—every good ideologue knows this well." And he said this with his index finger up as though gifting Cezal a kernel of wisdom. "My oasis will dry up and eventually be forgotten. After a while, the winds of time will erode the names of even the most famous among us until they are dust indiscernible from the rest of the desert. That will be my fate just as much as yours. Part of the power of ideology, however, is that it grounds you in the present. There are many ideologues of antiquity who used ideologies that ground you in the future— past your own life. But those I despise. They sell you the future in exchange for accepting an unsatisfactory present. It's pure, unimpeded escapism." Zamen paused, raised his eyebrow, and started shaking his head. "You want to know what evil is, Cezal, that's it. They steal your life from you and make you thank them for it. But I'm getting off-topic and am talking too much. You, Cezal, sound like the kind of person who's unsatisfied with his life. What are you doing here, really?"

Cezal paused and thought for a moment before beginning to respond. He honestly wasn't sure what he was doing, he explained. His companion, however, saw his effort and nonetheless praised him subtly for at least getting out there and trying to make his life better.

A couple of weeks passed, and Zamen and Cezal became increasingly connected. They usually took their breakfast and dinner together, and often various passengers would come over to join them, a sort of *open-door policy* seemingly having developed. Zamen was stubbornly present with each passenger when talking or in any way engaging with them. When you talked with Zamen, you were the only person in the world. Add to this, he always seemed to know what to do and say, and it's easy to see how he made himself quite a few friends in such a short time. Cezal often vaguely wondered why Zamen hung around someone such as himself. As for the scenery, they had finally left the endless forest, and now it was gently sloping hills covered with various grasses and shrubbery. Much was turning brown in the oncoming autumn, and the sky thus became the most striking feature of the region, with the clouds, often wispy and unsubstantial, floating with speed, high in the sky. On longer stops, Zamen and Cezal would often venture off the train for a couple of hours to see the various villages and buy more food from the vendors for whom the train guaranteed a constant supply of customers. On one such occasion, while they walked around, among the wood houses with light-blue gables, the autumn sky seemed to fill the world, and the crispness of the air filled them in turn.

The day being as nice as it was, they stopped at a small café with redwood paneling and, after ordering, sat outside at a rickety wooden table next to the side street, cobbled not with the seemingly customary gray stones, but rather with an assortment of slightly larger, rounder stones of various colors, the most common of which seemed to be a sort of reddish-brown. While it made for nice aesthetic appeal, when carriages came around, it seemed rather uncomfortably bumpy.

Over their coffees, which came in delightful ceramic cups decorated in the Delft style, they began a conversation.

Zamen looked up from his cup. "I've been thinking about my ideology more, and if I'm able to make it something that does help the people, it would be a shame for it to end after my death, don't you think?"

Cezal took a sip. "I suppose so."

"Well," replied the ideologue, "I've been thinking more about it, and I think I'll include purity in the ideology."

A bemused smile spread over Cezal's face. "What do you mean, 'include purity in the ideology?'"

"Well," clarified Zamen, "I mean just that. I'll come up with a way to have right and wrong actions so those who do the 'wrong' actions will be seen as impure."

Cezal furrowed his eyebrows. "Don't all societies then have the concept of purity? There's no place you could go where everything is permissible. And besides, by virtue of having an ideology in the first place, a system of morality will naturally arise. There's no way to get out of that."

Zamen stared into his cup for a moment. "That's true, yes," he began. "But there are ways to use 'permissibility' as a tool instead of a naturally developing phenomenon—of course, I'll have to work around the local culture and the moral interpretation of my ideology. But if I create some rules that I say are necessary for being a good person, but which aren't *actually* necessary for living in a healthy society, then it creates a better *in* and *out* group, so the ideology can be more visible and more easily used as part of someone's identity."

He paused a moment, and they both watched a barley-filled cart clop its way down the street. "Or even better yet, I can make it be something almost all people do or want to do, so then it's not even about whether you *actually* commit that offense, but whether the proper person accuses you of committing that offense. My initial thought is having sex, but that comes with far too much baggage. Maybe something more along the lines of getting power would be better. Yes, that would certainly help me not to have rivals. But I wonder if it would make people too docile." He continued to talk to himself, and Cezal just watched him with relative interest. "And too, it would make people judgmental, which as you know I find quite annoying. I don't know. Maybe there should be more of a *debt* people have instead. Yes! That's it. It's easy to make people feel indebted, and it gives them a sense of purpose too. Perhaps then, I'll say there's a certain debt we have to the world, a debt of existence, as it were. What do you think of that eh, Cezal?" he said, raising his eyebrow in a playfully mischievous way.

Cezal nodded. "Well, it's certainly an idea, and I think it is more elegant to have purity through debt than by addressing it head-on. I thought you don't like purity, though? Don't you think this may be getting a bit outside of the scope of what you're really trying to do?"

He took a nonchalant sip as he shook his head. "No, I don't think so. After all, if you can't make your ideology self-perpetuate, it has a far more limited impact. It's useful to think of each ideology as being a certain kind of animal. All of them exist in some kind of environment and have their own niche. There's a certain *survival-of-the-fittest-ness* about it. If someone's ideology is far more aggressive than someone else's, then that ideology will, in a manner of speaking, start to kill out the other. Obviously, I'm oversimplifying it quite a bit, but you get the general idea. As for purity, it's a useful concept. There's no problem with it as long as the ideologue themself doesn't actually believe in it." He said this all rather matter-of-factly and took another sip of the coffee before leaning back to take in the bright blue sky.

Cezal shook his head lightly. "I don't know, Zamen. I think you're going down a precarious path. You said yourself that it's a very thin line, no? If you continue, I think your ideology will be more about the perpetuation of power than the betterment of the people."

Zamen paused a second. "Hm, yes, perhaps. I'll keep thinking on it."

They took to enjoying their coffees and people watching. In the brisk weather, most people wore coats and patterned scarves of some kind or another, often with vibrant floral patterns or dull browns and grays. They walked in the slow way people in small towns always seem to.

After some minutes, Zamen broke their trance. "Yes, I suppose you do have a point. It's important for an ideologue not to get too big for their britches, as it were. Like I said the other night, that's part of the reason I dislike myself. I do it on purpose. Perhaps it could be said to be under a sort of veil of universal misanthropy, so I can only dislike myself so much. I know I'm not important enough to be worth feeling anything about too intensely. But it is a good tool to remind one of one's place," he shrugged.

"I suppose it can be," replied Cezal. "But is such a method *really* necessary?"

"Well…" began Zamen, drawing out the word in an attempt to seem equivocal. "It's not essential, perhaps, but it's certainly useful. And there's some grounding for it too. It's not just one of those empty concepts." He leaned forward again to take another sip. "You know, after uncovering oneself, and uncovering oneself again, and repeating the process a few scores more, one comes to meet the true emptiness of one's being." At this point, Zamen began to use more animated gesticulation, making ample use of his arms to punctuate the proper points of emphasis. "It seems to me like most people are somewhat despaired by this discovery, but really, all it means is that nothing matters. That there isn't really anything. Just like I said the other night—it's just to say one shouldn't take things too seriously, because what *is* there to take seriously. To that same end, one is better off not romanticizing their condition. It just makes it harder to improve oneself and change for the better. And that's just another thing the misanthropy is good for." He paused a second to see Cezal's reaction. He appeared interested.

"You know," Zamen continued, "when I was a teenager, I knew a guy who lived in my hometown, just down the street from me. We never were that close, but *living* so close to one another, we shared friends and often ended up with the same crowd. He grew up in a rather controlling household. His father was something of a patriarch, and the mother rather passive—more shadow than a person, as my friend himself once said with disgust during one of his more rebellious periods. Regardless, his dad was something of a man-about-town with many social obligations in addition to running the local paper, which, in our town of around 80,000 people, was sizable enough for the profits therefrom to make them considerably affluent—a high-profile family to say the least."

Zamen paused a second to stare at a particularly striking cloud floating in the sky behind Cezal.

"Well anyhow, I myself have never done well with authoritarian figures and was largely left to my own devices as a kid, so the anecdotes my friend would tell us every once in a while, or the excuses he'd have for not being able to come out, evoked what would, for me, be a very suffocating home life. He, while naturally not being horribly excited about it, seemed to manage well enough. Nonetheless, as time went on, we all graduated from school. Some headed off to the big city to go to university, others started working full-time or doing something or another, but he seemed to have stagnated. I came back the summer before my last year of university, where I was studying journalism of all things." Zamen saw Cezal's look of modest surprise. "I don't look like the type to have gone to university for journalism?" Zamen asked. "I would have thought my cheap suit and loquaciousness would have all but given it away," he chuckled. "Anyhow, I was back in my town that summer and, for old times sake, we met up, just the two of us and went into the forest with some sausage, beer, and fixings for a campfire. It got later and later, and while I could drink a fair amount and not really get that drunk, he was quite the opposite. As the night wore on, he started crying and going into how he was such a coward. I've always hated that word."

Cezal looked at Zamen quizzically. "What do you mean?"

"It's not the concept I have a problem with," Zamen quickly corrected, "but just how it sounds. I try to avoid using the term as much as I can. But regardless, my friend went on and on about how he couldn't live, and how he failed, and what a disappointment he was. By this point in my life, I hadn't learned when to stop drunk people from wallowing in their sorrows and when to let them vent, so this all continued for felt like at least an hour, by which point it was twilight, and the sky was this brilliant red. It looked really quite striking through the trees.

"I remember my friend stuttering out at one point as he sat crumpled with his back against a log that he hated himself, or something to that end. It was pretty sad to hear. He didn't even really say it to me, but more to himself, as though it were something he were finally coming to terms with. So we sat in silence for a few more minutes, staring into the dying fire. Without a word, he smashed one of the beer bottles against a log and made to stab his throat with it.

"Luckily, I had seen where this was going and had been watching him closely. I knew the direction he was heading down in the minutes leading up to his smashing the bottle, but I guess I wanted to see if he'd *actually* try to do something." Cezal sat back and crossed his legs. "I was able to wrestle the bottle away from him easily enough and threw it out into the darkness of the forest. I then did my best to offer some encouraging words, though I can't claim to have been all that good with that sort of thing. But it seemed to have worked well enough and we sat in silence for a while, staring again into the fire and listening to the sounds of the light wind through the pine trees.

"After things felt calm long enough, I asked him what he was thinking about. Upon hearing no response, looked at him. His eyes didn't have the intention or intensity as they had when he had broken the bottle, but looked wearier instead.

"He finally responded, and maybe it was the interaction that gave him more energy at that moment, but he seemed to gain a bit of vigor. He asked me what would it take for him to just leave—just run off into the sunset to some new town.

"When he told me that, I sighed a bit and shook my head up-and-down lightly while looking into the fire to make it seem like I was pondering his words. I told him he could do that, but that one's problems have a way of finding you wherever you are. In short, I told him he couldn't escape his troubles My advice had been incomplete, and I knew it, but I couldn't think of anything better to say. In response, my friend just continued staring into the flames."

Cezal continued to look at Zamen, entranced by the story.

"After a few more minutes," Zamen continued, "I said we should probably get headed home. So I got up and stamped out the little there was left of the fire, poured a bottle of river water onto the embers, and then covered it with dirt. As I was doing this, he quickly broke another beer bottle, but as I was preoccupied, I wasn't as attentive as I had been before, and only realized what he was doing from the sound of another bottle's smash. With one swift thrash, he made a deep, long cut in his forehead.

"I ran over to take the bottle from him, asking him what the hell he was thinking. Surprisingly, my friend offered no resistance and just leaned back on the log again. A little, dopey smile was on his face as blood spilled down.

"He mumbled something I couldn't quite catch, but his expression was almost euphoric. Eventually, he composed himself enough to assure me that he was okay. I just looked at him for a bit with a half-confused, half-disgusted expression and then moved on, glad he didn't seem to be planning on doing anything more at least."

"What's going through your head when you do something like that?" Zamen asked rhetorically, shaking his head in Cezal's direction before continuing. "I figured maybe it was a way of proving to himself he wasn't a complete coward and he was free. But regardless of why, the thing is, he thought he was important enough to hate—important enough to warrant killing. It was crazy!" Zamen threw up his arms. "But regardless, it's certainly a night I've remembered." Cezal looked somewhat askance at Zamen by this point.

"I ended up taking him back," the ideologue continued. "Made sure his wound was clotting and that he wouldn't bleed out overnight. I knew once his parents found out about what happened, they'd be furious. I assumed he'd tell them it was an accident, which I assumed would help his case. Though," he tilted his head to the side, "with them, I guess I really didn't know. They were probably more upset about the scar than the reasons for it."

"Anyhow," Zamen continued, "I made it a point not to see him again the rest of the summer, but made sure to inform his friends of what happened. They didn't seem too surprised at any point until I told them about the forehead part—that caught them off guard. Anyhow, I knew they were all caring enough they wouldn't just forget about him, so I felt okay to leave it be after that. Maybe that's one of my shortcomings, "Zamen mused. "I like to leave things before they really come to a conclusion. I don't like to really know the ending. I think it comes from this romanticized, pseudo-nostalgic desire for ambiguity. I like things better when they're not completely defined. Whether this is a virtue or not, I don't really know. I'd guess it's not, but I don't think it's that big of a deal either way. Anyhow," he shrugged, "I never saw nor heard from him again. He wasn't there the next summer I was back in my town, so I assume he moved away or died or something."

Cezal, his coffee now finished, looked at Zamen, leaning in with his eyebrows raised.

"Oi," replied Zamen, "don't look so disapproving of my apathy on the subject. I told you this story to exemplify the ways in which people think they're more important than they actually are. My acquaintance who sliced his forehead did so out of such intense emotion. The pressure was all built up, and he didn't know how to properly deal with it, so he released it in such a way." Zamen leaned forward and put his elbows on the table with his palms outstretched, raised halfway up. "He didn't realize he wasn't important enough to hate. But aside from that as well, it goes to show the power of ideology. Make no mistake, Cezal, ideology's not just something for kings and religious leaders—all of us have an ideology. My friend's family certainly had one. One I didn't respect—driven by vanity and guilt and honor and all those wasteful things. My point is that my ideology will have a different set of values, a different set of pressures. It'll create among the people a different understanding of self. It will value things like compassion, honesty, and self-overcoming."

"Well, that's an interesting idea," Cezal replied. "I suppose I see more what you mean."

Before there was time for Cezal to give a more meaningful response, Zamen took out his watch. "Oh my, look at the time," he said. "We'd better get going if we're to make our train."

And off they went.

* * *

Nearly nightfall some days later, both Cezal and Zamen were in the cabin reading their books at the table between their two beds. The cabin was filled with the clack of the train, and the warmth leftover from the afternoon sun.

Zamen set down his book in a manner that was almost dramatic.

"You know, Cezal, it seems to me most people live in fear of others in some base way. They have this pervasive anxiety that follows them at all times. So much so they don't even realize it's there until it's not. Fear for the future. Fear of other people's opinions. Fear of letting others down—or rather, that they will be seen as a disappointment. Wouldn't you agree? But in the end, we are completely alone, and no one can save us from death or sadness. And so, why do we care so much for the thoughts of others?"

Cezal took a somewhat annoyed breath in. "Is there something you're trying to imply by asking me this question in such a straightforward way?"

"No, it's just been on my mind. Don't get so defensive."

"Mm. You're right," agreed Cezal, putting his book down and clasping his hands. "Yes, I suppose people do have this fear, don't they? This *anxiety*. Well, what can I say? I suppose most people think themselves weak, don't they?"

"Perhaps so. Do you think they're weak?" He looked at Cezal.

"I don't know. I feel inclined to say yes. How often do people rise to the occasion? I think our age is lacking in situations to which one can rise."

Zamen gave a light chuckle. "Well, that's a rather defeatist attitude, wouldn't you say? I think it would seem, to someone who hasn't rocked the boat, that there are few occasions to rise to. Perhaps, really, that's the best measure of whether someone has been living too cautiously. If you seek to be more, to be greater than you were the day before, then naturally, you will come into obstacles. In fact, I'd say if you're not facing obstacles, you're wasting your time—you're failing to develop yourself."

Cezal stared out the window. "Hm… well, I suppose that sounds right. Perhaps so—perhaps that is a part or even a major part. What do people become when not challenged?"

"Yes, they become weak. Like muscles of a body in disuse, their spirit atrophies."

"I suppose so," Cezal replied, already deep in thought and trying not to feel defensive. They stared out the window and watched the scenery passing them by.

* * *

At one of the stations the train arrived to, there was a man with a wide-brimmed, straw hat and a sturdy cane, presumably waiting for someone. As the train had come to a stop, he had taken a telegram paper out of his breast pocket and verified the car number and waited, looking evenly between the two exits of the car as the passengers filed out. It was a sunny, picturesque day—likely one of the last of the year. The days were getting noticeably shorter. In fact, although the train arrived at the station only a little after 3:00 p.m., the sun was already in the lowest quartile of the sky and obscured the mountains it overlooked. The man continued looking as the passengers kept going out, his eyes squinting in the afternoon light. Zamen watched him rather intently. Finally, a young boy came out and went to him and gave him a hug. The man hugged him back, and they began to walk away. A kind smile spread over Zamen's face, almost a longing one. He noticed Cezal saw the scene too.

"It's lovely, isn't it?" Zamen remarked. "There's something so nice about the childhood love for family. The dynamic changes as you get older, I suppose, so it isn't quite the same. I guess one realizes their parents and grandparents aren't quite the perfect beings they once thought they were. No longer are they the bastions of all that is wonderful about the world."

Cezal shrugged. "I suppose so. It is quite nice, the kind of pure, naïve love the fortunate ones have as a child." Cezal sat back and sighed. "Yes, it's a sort of love for the world, isn't it? If you're such a child, you don't really discern evil." He paused a bit as they watched the people milling about outside. "Say, Zamen, your ideology, do you think it will help ultimately, or do you think it will serve to make children lose their innocence more quickly?"

Zamen sighed and leaned back.

"I don't know," he admitted. "But innocence isn't everything either. You wouldn't look kindly upon a man in his thirties thinking the world to be all pancakes and lemon zest."

"Mm, yes, I suppose so," Cezal replied.

The train began to lug forward with all the commotion and noise that necessarily came along.

Cezal began to daydream, looking out the window at the quaint summer town. It existed quite nicely this time of day.

Some minutes later, Zamen interjected, "You make a good point."

Cezal looked at him absentmindedly. "What do you mean?"

"Your question about innocence and ideology," he replied.

"Oh, that. I didn't realize you'd let it preoccupy you so long," Cezal said. "Are you not confident that your ideology will be a force for good?"

Zamen narrowed his eyes. "Oh please, Cezal, people care too much nowadays about seeming confident. Anyone too preoccupied with seeming so needs to get their priorities in order." He cleared his throat. "Yes, I'm confident in myself, but that doesn't mean I don't hesitate or am closed to changing a plan, time permitting. And either way, you're not in my target audience. I don't have to worry about putting on airs around you. Yes, see, that's the problem." He put both elbows on the table between Cezal and him and began his gesticulating. "People have become too shallowly self-aware. It's almost as though they have made themselves into their own caricature." Cezal looked at him perplexed. "I'm not being very clear," The ideologue continued. "For example, what I loathe most is those who talk of a *personal brand*. Oh, how I hate that concept so. They're objectifying themselves and think they're slick in doing so! They think *they're* being the ideologue, Cezal! It's crazy! It's times like that when I wonder what people are doing with their lives. It's almost like they don't need some malevolent ideologue to take their power away from them: no, they do it just fine on their own."

"How do you mean?" Cezal asked.

Zamen began to get frenzied, waving his arms around and running his hands through his hair every-so-often. "I mean that people are dehumanizing themselves! They're viewing themselves increasingly as a product and then wonder why they feel so alienated from everything. It never ceases to amaze me how it seems people almost *want* to con-sign themselves to being victims of circumstance—self-com-modification is really just the most modern iteration of self-victimization that I've seen. A more classic way, if you would, is through purity, though I suppose that's a bit more complex. But rest assured: it's just as caustic to the well-being of the people.

Cezal chuckled a bit and adjusted how he sat. "And what do you mean—how is purity so bad?"

"Oh, Cezal, don't get me started!" And Zamen laughed a bit. "I hate those who hold purity in high regard. I don't think there is a more diluted and vile lot of people in the whole world. Be good. Don't be evil. Do this; don't do that.

My god, how they whine and complain while asserting their self-righteousness. Those who stand tall and lord their purity over the heads of the heathens—fire fills their eyes. It is the fire of unbearable arrogance. They manage to be simultaneously weak and yet influential. It's pitiful. They are less people than they are tar-pits in human form. Don't get too close, or you'll fall in and get scalded." Zamen leaned back, and a sickly smile spread over his face. "Ah yes, but they got one thing right. I must give credit where credit is due. They know how to evoke guilt. Ah yes, guilt." And he looked at Cezal with a glint in his eye, his upper lip quivering ever so slightly. "It's a beautiful concept, really. Evil perhaps, but beautiful, sort of the same way an infectious disease is. Yes, a sickening beauty. Perhaps that's the best way to say it."

Cezal stared at him, his eyes somewhat widened.

"What? You seem taken aback," Zamen replied.

"I… well, it's just rather… I don't know, Zamen, it felt like there was something rather manipulative in you that you were letting shine through."

He gave a short laugh waved his arms in a dismissive way. "Ah, there's a part in us all that manipulates, Cezal. And besides, I've already told you that I think there's a part of me that's evil. Perhaps it comes to me easier, but at least it means that I know how to use it constructively." He pointed his finger knowingly as he said that. "I think you'll find that there's a certain evilness or sliminess to all ideologues. At the same time, not giving in to evil, but rather using it as a fuel to the fire of a better future: That's what marks the difference between a benevolent and malevolent ideologue. At all times, we walk on a knife. A sharper knife means a better ideology. Should we manage to walk the blade long enough without falling, a great future is all but guaranteed.

Ah," Zamen said, pointing again in that knowing way, "but that's the thing—love and hate, good and evil: all those grand, classic dichotomies—they're less different than one would think. You'd be surprised how often people simply get swept away by intensity and are simultaneously filled with both. Don't you think?"

Cezal, again, stared at him, a little more blankly this time than taken aback. The train clacked, and the afternoon sun was drifting inside in golden heaps, filling the room and making everything almost glow.

Finally, Cezal smiled a bit, and in realizing the thread of the conversation had already been lost, decided to poke fun at Zamen. "You think rather highly of yourself, don't you?" Cezal asked.

Zamen smiled back and laughed a bit, throwing his head up in the process. "Yes, I suppose you could say that. I'm surprised you're just now mentioning it. But I also know I'm not special. I just realized my potential more than most people do. And the thing is, all ideologues have a pretty big ego. We have to admit that, but really, it's our ego for which we are ultimately celebrated. We say what everybody's thinking, and we do what everybody wishes they had the courage to do. We live, and we have power. If the people feel like we are on the same team, then we're golden.

"Too often, through defensiveness and ego, it becomes all about power, or rather, it becomes apparent that all along, it was only about power. The longer people seem to have it, the further they seem to get from being human. They lose their grip on reality. Ah, but my friend, there's nothing quite like it. Not that I've had many occasions to experience it firsthand, but I'll make sure I do." Zamen nodded. "And I'll do my best not to lose my grip on reality. I will, I'm sure, to some extent, but I'll keep reminding myself I'm not special. That's where the self-hate comes from. Or perhaps hate is too strong of a word. It would be better said that an ideologue needs to hold a good deal of misanthropy for the entire world and apply that same level of misanthropy to themself. That way, you keep yourself in check, but at the same time, you think, I don't trust *anyone else* to do the job right either." He threw his arms up. "Ah, I don't know. Perhaps that's simply too far into the future. I should focus more on the present. Because all I can say at this point is that whatever happens, I know the life I have now is about to end forever, and I try to savor that, I do. In many ways, this train ride is the epilogue to my former life, like the calm before the storm. Criticize me if you want for romanticizing my life as I'm in the process of living it, but I can tell you, it makes it far more interesting to live."

Cezal chuckled and leaned back and laid down on his bed, his brown clothes contrasting with the afternoon glow of the seldom-washed, formerly white sheets. His feet, still clad with his brown leather shoes, were propped up on the wall facing the window. A smile spread over his face. "Yes, well, I suppose you're right. It does make it more interesting."

6

The following day, the dull purple glow of dawn painted over the increasing steppelike landscape. Over a breakfast of hard-boiled eggs, bread, and tea, Cezal got to asking Zamen more about the world of ideologues, and the subculture that would naturally grow out of it.

Zamen smiled at the question and seemed to be excited to share.

"Well, you see," he began, "it's not as though we are a coordinated group. There are no ideologue conventions or publications. That said, however, there are two main *camps*, if you will, that most ideologues prescribe to." He pushed his plate to the side and began using his arms to explain things. "The first camp believes the ideology itself can be an end goal. For example, such ideologues could believe in the inherent validity of ideas like nationalism, classicism, racism, culturalism, and so on. They are called *intrinsic ideologues*, because they believe, or convince themselves to believe, there to be something at the 'core' of humans that forms their identity, and that these *isms*, if you wish to so call them, are a valid way of getting to the heart of that human identity. The other main camp of ideologues is called, aptly, *extrinsic ideologues*. They believe there is nothing deeper than the material world and that the ideals that intrinsic ideologues hold are misplaced and erroneous. Extrinsic ideologues think the other camp is, in short, weak because they feel the need to hold onto the ideas of social position, culture, nationality, or what have you in order to properly define themselves. As you could probably guess, I am an extrinsic ideologue."

Cezal nodded his head slowly and folded his barely used handkerchief. "I see," he said, taking a sip of tea. "You seem to hold some pretty strong views on intrinsic ideologues to be so categorically saying they're weak. Is there more to that?"

Zamen paused a second, and it was clear he had a speech well-laid out, and it was simply a matter of where to start that gave him a slight pause. "Well, yes, I would say there's a quite valid reason for my near-universal condemnation of intrinsic ideologues. Perhaps to help you understand more why I loathe them so, it would help to start with an example of the type of intrinsic ideologue that I, at the very least, respect. Because," he said, raising his finger, "there is only one kind of intrinsic ideologue who is worth anyone's time and who is anything more than just a swindler. That is, the kind of intrinsic ideologue who *dies* for their beliefs. In doing so, they make their lives the ideology itself. It is a very beautiful thing—the elegant unification of belief and action.

"In truly trying times, when people have little to live for, and the future is bleak, it is more common to find these types of ideologues. They may not create vast movements and topple regimes, but they are an ideologue for their own life and perhaps family and community. This type is far more common in such trying times because it is then when humans are forced to face the reality of their existence in a much more direct way. Because, at the end of the day, even when everything is taken from you, you can still give your life. That's the basic principle behind being a martyr. However, these martyrs are almost always quickly forgotten and never did much in their own life either. An intrinsic ideologue, however, who gives their life to their ideology and who still amasses wide support in their lifetime: That person is rare indeed and embodies a *pure* ideology that happens only once in a hundred years."

Cezal looked at him somewhat withdrawn and with furrowed eyebrows. "Well, hold on," he said. "You can't just romanticize death like that."

Zamen squinted at him. "Well, I don't see why not, but either way," he said, waving his arms dismissively. "Hold on. You misunderstand me. One thing is it's not that I romanticize death when I talk about the martyrs. For them, I merely describe the principle behind it. You would agree, would you not, that if a martyr weren't to die for some hopeless cause, they wouldn't still be considered a martyr?"

"Well," replied Cezal, "they're not always hopeless causes that—"

"Yes, yes," Zamen interrupted. "I know. But they're at least hopeless for the martyr themselves, and it's only through some deep, grand faith that the martyr thinks their sacrifice will ever amount to anything. Do you see what I mean?"

Cezal slid his mouth slightly to the side. "Yes, I suppose so. But the way you talk about these intrinsic ideologues who die for their ideology. Certainly you can see how you romanticize them."

Zamen paused a second, shook his shoulders slightly, and put his lips out in the way people do when they mean to indicate, "And so?"

"Yes," continued Zamen. "I suppose so. Though, I'm not romanticizing the act of suicide, but rather the fatalistic notion of meaning. It's almost that there's a sort of sick poetic justice when people die for their beliefs. When people make that ultimate sacrifice for ideology, it means they *truly* believe it with the entirety of their being. It's rather misguided, the entire notion, but it's perhaps with smug satisfaction that I can respect such ideologues. They may be useless fuckheads." He let out a satisfied sigh. "But they are pure in thought and action, and that is something to respect."

Cezal shook his head a bit. "I think I'll have to disagree with you there. I don't see this value of martyrdom you speak of. It sounds even rather depraved, I would say."

Zamen stared at him for a moment. The train kept clacking, and the sparse scrub of the outer world continued to pass by. "Perhaps so. There may be some depravity there. But to make sure you really understand my point, because I think it is quite an important one, let me give you an example. There is a town some five hundred kilometers southwest of the last town we stopped in, where they had been *very* nationalist. They saw themselves as superior, and indeed, they had a lot of power. They were the largest city in the area and enjoyed a great many technologies and wealth. In effect, they ruled over that whole region."

Cezal nodded and took a bite of the egg.

"Well, anyhow, they acted as any state would, trying to get more power and getting perhaps a bit too bigheaded for their own good. Of course, this almost invariably begets arrogance and sloppiness. A skilled local ideologue, however, was able to see that their little empire was on the decline, and so, in order to save it from itself, she began to speak of their superior technology and nationality. As time went on, the pride and arrogance of the people grew and grew, and they regarded anyone who disagreed with the ideologue as being against the city's best interest. Now, normally, such an intrinsic ideologue would be reviled by extrinsic ideologues—and indeed, at first, she was. But, as time went on, we started to see she raised the people's pride to a level that almost left the realm of the real world. The narrative she got the people to believe was itself larger-than-life. She got them to see their city as the bastion of all that was good in the world and the outside as filled with evil—in need either of being saved or of being avoided altogether."

Zamen nodded to himself. "You know, I think it is now safe to say, deep down, this ideologue hated the people there—likely hated all of humanity. But her hate *exceeded* itself. Her hate became devotion. Or maybe the other way around. Either way, she began to achieve something near sublime. Eventually, the people were so feverous and filled with adoration and hate they forgot who they were. Their individual identities began to melt away into a collective, burbling pot of narrative, emotion, and purity. They began to act erratically: people began to punch walls and ram their heads into doors to feel the pain, they consistently over-ate, they had violent sex, they drove those who weren't fervent believers out of town, and they slaughtered their animals not by simply cutting their necks, but by smashing them. She was so skillful that she got them to reach such a point of devolution and crazed fervor she was able to give one last, crushing sermon. In this sermon, atop a mountain, she called upon the people to finally seize their glory—to fully embrace their betterness and reach the sublime. 'But,' she said, 'the sublime can only be reached in contradiction because it is in contradiction that we are most whole. And so, we must kill ourselves. It must be violent and bloody, and it must be done. Only we can do it, for the sake of humanity, because we are so better, because we are so much more, because we must be the saviors. It is the only way. It is the golden way. It is the *sublime* way.' And with that, according to those who recount the story, the eyes of the people gleamed like they had never gleamed before, and she knew then they were no longer people, but rather vessels for ideology."

Cezal gave a deprecatory half-smile. "What is this story, Zamen?"

He waved his arms dismissively. "Well, hold on, Cezal, let me finish. So she led them, down from the mountain, to a cliff edge. And there, she commanded they all jump. 'Jump for glory! Jump for transcendence! Jump because that is what you were born to do!' And so they did—all however-many-hundreds of people there were. It was, of course, not complete, for the children did not understand and were scared and didn't want to jump. They were too young to understand and lose themselves to ideology. But enough were so enraptured that they dragged the children with them—screaming in terror as they looked at the carnage and saw where they were heading. As the cliff drop wasn't *so* great, upon falling, many of the people were simply hurt but nowhere near dead, so they began to kill each other down there. They would move the body of their fallen uncle off their leg and crawl to bludgeon their neighbor, who would return the favor. To call it brutal would be an understatement, of course, but that is how they ended. At last, the ideologue looked down at the carnage— the bodies, the blood, the dust, and moaning, and threw herself off the cliff, dying on impact. And that was the end."

Cezal looked at Zamen with apprehension, having drawn his arms toward the edge of the table and leaning back. "I…

well, Zamen, I don't really know how one is supposed to react to that story. It's rather horrifying."

"Well, yes, in it, you can see some of the worst of humanity. That's true. I apologize. One often gets dulled to the shock value of the things one deals with, but yes, it is quite a tragic tale. From an educational, if clinical, view, certainly though, you can see the value of the story."

Cezal paused and gave him a slight look of reproach. "Mm… yes… I suppose so."

"I actually went to visit that town after hearing news of their mass-suicide, or rather, *rapture*. It was a beautiful place, with lush, green rolling hills dotted with wildflowers leading up to the mountains. The town was spread out, and the houses were made of white limestone, and the doors were painted a vibrant blue. In fact, the town had been previously known for their special houses built in this style. But now, of course, it was empty. Not a soul was there. I saw a memorial put up in honor of the people who lost their lives for ideology. It was a strange sight because it was evident that this had become a place of pilgrimage for other people attempting to attain *the sublime*, but as well, there were others who desecrated the monument, and understandably so," he sighed. "However, you feel about the issue, though, one thing is for sure, it'll leave you with a sense of awe… And *that*, my friend, is the power of ideology."

Cezal looked at him still with a facial expression as though he had just eaten something bitter. "I must say, Zamen, that is still a rather disconcerting story."

"Well, yes, it's certainly not something one recounts to extol the virtues of the modern world. Ah, but other than the children, one can't feel bad for such people."

"And why is that?" Cezal probed.

Zamen looked at him as though thickheaded and sighed, as though a parent telling their child a beloved relative wouldn't be able to visit that year over the winter holiday.

"Look, Cezal," he said, leaning in, resting his elbows on the table with his palms faced semi-up. "These people, they let themselves get taken advantage of. They were too stupid for their own good. If you're going to act like a buffalo—a beast of burden—when you could have actually used your head, then don't be surprised when you get herded off a cliff like one. At that point, really, it's for your own good. Let that be a lesson, Cezal, because no one thinks they're the buffalo, but if you look around you and all you see is other buffalo, then chances are you're part of the herd. All this shit people spout about liberalism and individual rights—it's just that: shit." He shook his head. "People will say they believe in it when it's convenient to do so, but as soon as the going gets tough, everyone forgets about the *values* they claim to hold so dear. It's about power, Cezal. That's all it's ever been. So be prepared. Especially in a democracy, most people have more power than they should."

Cezal squinted and leaned back. "Well, hold on, Zamen. I get that democracy is not perfect, but certainly, it's far better than a dictatorship or something of the sort?"

Zamen put both his hands up. "Yes. Yes, it's true. One wouldn't want to conflate things that shouldn't be conflated. But people take such a self-satisfied, smug view of democracy. Those born into it take it for granted. Those who actually appreciate it do so because they understand the alternative. But see, that's the problem. It's almost a paradox: once you establish democracy, people grow weary of it and become lazy, looking to give up their freedom, too naïve to the patterns of history for their own good. That's why an ideologue should be a sort of benevolent dictator—though, of course, they would never refer to themselves as one."

"And how often are they successful, these benevolent dictators?" Cezal asked.

"Well, usually they're not," admitted Zamen. "Power has a way of getting to you, and unscrupulous people have a knack for amassing power and winning the favor of the people."

Cezal looked at him squarely. "And what makes you think you're different?"

Zamen gave a light laugh. "You raise a good point, Cezal. If I don't keep myself in check, I could very well end up like the majority of despots throughout history, assuming I'm even successful in the first place."

* * *

A couple of evenings later, as Zamen was out hobnobbing with some other passengers on the train, Cezal sat down on his own to a nice dinner of broiled herring and applesauce—something that, the chef had assured him, was quite difficult to procure whilst being so far away from both the nearest apple orchards and the sea. He nibbled at his food, drowning the taste when he could with burnt coffee. It was pleasant enough, though, with the train clacking gently as it always did.

After a bit of time, another figure entered the dinner car—the ever-worn and joy-devoid Bekochan, who wandered aimlessly down the aisle, toward Cezal's general direction. It seemed Bekochan had taken somewhat of a liking to Cezal. His fetid body odor was often what announced his presence when he would join him during his late-night coffees. At times, Cezal asked himself if he really enjoyed Bekochan's company or if it was more really an inconvenience. He had, of course, met people who suck the energy out of you and leave you feeling a deep gloominess after being in their presence for any longer than a few moments. But Bekochan wasn't quite like this. Granted, he wasn't a happy figure by any measure and was rather unpleasant to look at, but he needed company, and who was Cezal to deny him that? It didn't bother him all that much most of the time.

The impromptu companion was always rather a *wildcard* in that you would never know how lucid or not he would be. At times, he appeared before Cezal, a sobbing mess who could barely string two thoughts together. At other times, he was clearly not sober but still capable of intelligent conversation, and at other times still, he would appear sober, a cloud of melancholy most often trailing not too far behind. This night, as it so happened, was to be one of his less lucid ones.

Once he wandered close enough, and his disorientation became apparent to Cezal, he waved him over. "Bekochan!… Bekochan!" Cezal yelled in a subdued way.

He looked over.

"Hey, why don't you come sit with me, eh? I'll bring you some coffee."

He wandered over vacantly, pouring himself into his seat and resting his head on the table, his arms underneath.

Cezal regarded the sad sap. "Okay, Bekochan, would you like some coffee?"

No response.

"Okay, I'm going to get you some coffee and water, eh, don't move. You should drink some—you'll feel better."

A couple of minutes later, Cezal came back, the drinks in tow, and sat down to shake Bekochan up. He lifted his head meekly. "Here, drink some," Cezal offered.

They sat in silence for quite some time. Cezal relaxed with his coffee while staring out the window, which, by this point, acted more as just as a mirror for people watching, with the limited light from the train only dimly illuminating what appeared to be the blur of brown grass by the track. Beko-chan, sitting opposite to Cezal, his back to the rear door, kept his head up, staring as emptily as ever with his frail hands clasping the glass cup for warmth.

The standard drawn-out dinner scene played out in the car, and Bekochan and Cezal sat and watched it.

"I wish I could have been more."

Cezal looked over at the source of the broken silence.

"Why did I rebel against the world? What was there against which *to* rebel?" Bekochan was speaking in half-muttered phrases seemingly to himself, as though only thinking out loud. "Why did I try to teach the world? Why did I try to change things? Perhaps it is the ultimate form of apathy and defeat not to rebel." He continued to look into his cup of burnt coffee. "Those who do not rebel fade into the night never to be seen again, perhaps because they never were. When will I finally fade into the night?" He looked shortly up at Cezal like a puppy before looking down again. "I am a lost cause, my friend, a horrible cause. I can serve only as an example of what you should not become." He pursed his lips. "Fret not, because my life is not one most have. But it is one all *can* have. That is perhaps my lowly gift to the world: a warning. True living exists in the tension between things—in stretching oneself, in contradiction, going against one's own self-comfort, but don't make the same mistakes I did. Don't lose yourself too fully, because you can never go back. Sometimes it *is* too late." He paused awhile and sighed.

Cezal was at a loss for words from both the intensity and vagueness of what was just said.

"Ah, maybe I'm too hard on myself," Bekochan began, "but you know what bothers me most?" He looked into Cezal's eyes with a surprising and piercing presence. "I've yet to meet someone who has meant what they say. There's something about powerlessness and mediocrity, don't you think? I don't understand it."

"What do you mean?" Cezal asked.

Bekochan looked at his tablemate, sighed, and looked into his cup.

"I—" he shook his head. "It's no matter. I just… I wish I were more. I guess it's a lost cause, putting the weight of the world on yourself. But if you don't, who will? I guess that's where I fell short." He gave a light laugh. "It's never enough, is it? And how could it be? It's that obligation everyone has to the world, you know?"

Cezal, unsure of how to respond, did his best to give an understanding and reassuring smile. "I guess so."

The train kept clacking, and the scenery passed by as it always did. By then, most people had left, and there was only a light murmur as the waitstaff lackadaisically picked up dishes and cutlery.

* * *

Darkness in a room; alone. And at long last, Alja looked upon her body and saw it for what it was. She saw herself in her proper context. One with nature. Ah yes, with nature.

She mused. *The world is a resource, is it not?*

Alja nodded to herself in agreement. "Of course it is."

So you understand what you are then, right?

"Of course," she repeated.

So you understand then what you must do?

"I must be conquered. I must be spent."

So get to work.

* * *

The next morning was bright, and the world was painted with the sweet auburn sadness of autumn.

"What do you do when you're sad?" Cezal asked Zamen while mending a white sock that had developed a hole in the heel.

Zamen put down the newspaper he was reading. "Well," he shrugged, "I'm an ideologue, so I need to be careful about the feelings I express. Usually, they're fleeting, and I forget why I felt one way or another in a couple of days. Why? What do you do when you're sad?"

"I don't know. I've asked myself that for a while. I suppose sometimes all you can do is accept your sadness for what it is, and feel it at that moment."

"Well, yes, I suppose that's true. Though at the same time, one needn't dwell on such emotions," Zamen replied.

"I don't disagree with that," Cezal said, "but there is a difference between dwelling and repressing. Where exactly the line between one and the other is, I don't know."

Zamen nodded. "Yes, I suppose there's a level of truth to that, but one would be remiss to say there's no way to make a distinction. It is important that as much as possible, you not feel as though the object of your emotions—as though a victim of your own life. It seems those who have the tendency to repress, to their own detriment, reject their emotions in the moment; whereas those who don't have the inclination for repression are often more aptly described as *dwellers*. They likely have the tendency to, well, dwell, also to their own detriment. The balance is just a matter of what serves you better. There are some people I know who seem to enjoy melancholy. I don't really get it. It seems rather life-sucking if you ask me, but they seem to derive some kind of meaning from it."

"I suppose you're right. I've wondered about that too—the melancholy dwellers," Cezal mused, giving a small smile and with a twinkle in his eye to make sure Zamen wasn't taking himself too seriously. "I think I've found myself like that sometimes, and I've asked that same question too. I think it's because the sadness from melancholy and nostalgia is a certain type of mourning. And so to have those emotions means there's something worth mourning, however small or insignificant. And if something's worth mourning, then surely it must have had some meaning, wouldn't you say?"

Zamen gave an uncharacteristic, small smile and nodded his head. "Perhaps so," he replied before going back to reading.

* * *

One afternoon, they were sitting around. Cezal was staring out the window with a cup of barley tea, and Zamen was with his notebook out, reading a book while eating cottage cheese. Soon later, he turned the page, scanned it, and closed the book dramatically before looking directly at Cezal, who in turn caught his gaze with a raised eyebrow.

"I have a story to tell," Zamen said. There was a glimmer in his eye he always had when telling stories to break up the monotony.

Cezal smiled. "Do go on."

"For a couple of years, I lived far up north in the East, in the province above Sectohal. Over there, the rest of the world is far away, and the rules are different. Time there flows much more slowly, and information takes far longer to travel. Over there, the government is merely an abstract concept that bears little reality on people's day-to-day lives. There, the businesspeople are the ones who *really* run things. Money buys laws, morality, and even the privilege of existence." He ate a mouthful of cottage cheese and proceeded to point the spoon at Cezal for emphasis. "I'd really suggest you make your way up there someday. It's just a rather bizarre experience. Reality is *different* there in some palpable yet indescribable way. I wish I had a better way to explain it, but it's something one has to experience for themself. But anyhow, some years ago, I heard of a rich foreigner who, I suppose, would be considered an intrinsic ideologue. Though he was outside of the ideologue community and had no real background with us. But anyhow, this foreigner, he had a certain *vision for the world*, if you would—"

Cezal looked at him somewhat inquisitively, leaning back against the wall with one leg folded over the other. "Hold on, what do you mean by vision for the world?"

"Well," smiled Zamen, "although he had a background in business, I know he managed, surprisingly, to get some articles of his societal theory published in rather well-regarded journals; considering how much of an outsider he was, it's no small wonder." He shrugged. "I just know his main schtick was to say that the way humans are inclined to classify entities is incorrect, and we come to identify any entity by the characteristics that we see as inherent to it, its *quiddity*, to use the term he used. But really, he argued, there is no inherent characteristic in the first place. Really it is living things that define and create the world, and it's just that we all use largely the same biological processes to sense, and thus define, the world, so we come to generally hold the same understanding of reality. The view we have of the world, he argued, is valid, but no more so than any other view. According to him, there very likely are better ways of looking at the world—ways that are better conducive to a harmonious society or something like that."

Cezal looked at him, rather perplexed. "I think I somewhat follow what you're saying, but how can that idea be the basis for an entirely new society?"

Zamen replied quickly, "Yes, I see what you mean. It does have surprisingly widespread implications, though. For example, nowadays, with more and more technology, we humans have started to look at the world and nature increasingly as something that is conquerable, you know. Even take this train—the distance we are crossing would have taken multiple years by foot, I would think. And yet, if we were to have taken the fast one, we could have gotten to our destination in what, a couple of weeks maybe? The point is, nature is more and more an afterthought—a problem to be worked around, a resource at our disposal. And I agree with him there. No one respects the natural world anymore. It's really rather a shame. It's another reason people feel so empty nowadays.

"But I digress. Take the economy, for example. Think about how people talk about it. The language we use to describe it is the same kind of language we used to use to describe nature a few centuries ago. When you look at it that way, you can see we respect and see ourselves as the object of the economy far more than we do nature. The rich man, ironic as it is, was essentially saying that yes, it is valid to see the world in this way. Given the ways of the modern world, it certainly *logically* adds up. But we don't *have to* view the world in this way. And what he would say is that it is *healthier* not to view it in this way. So I suppose in short, his main point was just that we have full control over the narratives of our world, and these narratives will dictate more about our reality than reality dictates our narratives."

"Hmm, okay." Cezal nodded.

"Well, anyhow, he had lots of money, so he went to one of these remote cities and decided that starting with just a single town, he would create his own culture and nation based on this philosophical theory. He called his country *Davrara*. It had its own language, its own philosophical tradition, its own theory of economics—its own everything, really. And back then, many of the ideas were indeed quite modern, if a bit transgressive, though I suppose that was rather the point. Were he to have been successful, we would be living in quite a different world than we are today. Nonetheless, he was also rather perceptive and amassed quite the fortune through various means: Telegram companies, crop futures, vertical integration—yes, it was because of him that that term was popularized. So you know, stuff like that." Zamen waved his arms around as he spoke, his brown, disheveled hair moving as he did. "He was quite charismatic and knew how to get people on his side. It all was going well, and he had the support of money and those with power or influence in the area."

He looked at Cezal to see if he still appeared engaged. Cezal took a sip of coffee but nodded when he caught Zamen's eye.

"Well, anyhow," Zamen continued, "before he got to the city, one where corruption constantly stifled development, he started to give generous gifts to those in power there, passing it off as a gift for their future hospitality. They knew what he was doing, and that they were necessary for his success, so they received the gifts warmly. Then, a year or so later, once he actually arrived to the town, he made his presence known and threw a big party—extravagant by all measures. Many wondered why he was coming there—this rich Westerner." He took another bite of cottage cheese. "Ah, but soon they saw! He started picking up the slack that came about from the corruption and incompetence of the local and federal government: He funded schools, improved infrastructure, gave farmers better tools, and established everything in the Davrarian fashion. Because there was plenty of money behind it, the Davrarian way of things worked quite well, and the people liked it a lot. But the corrupt businessmen and officials he had been paying off were growing increasingly unhappy since this rich businessman had usurped them. He essentially took away their power and turned the people against them. They saw their necessity in Davraria as rapidly waning. But the Westerner, being one step ahead, managed to convey to them they were to join him and get a nice spot in the Davrarian government or face rather unpleasant alternatives. Most joined, and those who did not were quickly and quietly made an example of.

"With this well done, the people and those who used to have power were all on his side. Davraria began to expand, and people started to move to this new town in the East for the first time in generations. In short, all was well." He took another bite and nodded his head as he swallowed. "One day, however, a few years later, someone poisoned the rich man, and he died not an hour later. There was, of course, a period of chaos, but then things went back to normal." Zamen raised his eyebrows in a what-can-you-do way. "The rich man failed because he forgot something very important for an ideologue to remember. He forgot that, in the end, no matter how modern or cultivated the society is, one is *never* above brutality. One is always in a precarious situation. Our own bodies confine us and render us fragile. Even the greatest person in the whole world can be killed simply with a poisoned drink or in a freak accident. It takes nothing more."

Cezal looked at Zamen, the little remaining coffee in his cup now cold. "Hm, yes, that's a good point," Cezal replied. "It seems though that this example serves as a defeat to his philosophy too, wouldn't you say?"

"How so?" Zamen asked, leaning back.

"Well, perhaps not categorically so, but I would say it means he was looking upon the world in too clinical of a way. Yes, as the rich man said: the narratives of society are arbitrary, but we nonetheless structure our reality around them in such a way that makes the narratives self-perpetuating. They have an internal logic to them. Not only that, but I think it can be said most people *want* things to stay the same, or at least *feel* the same. They may want change when they can imagine it in a concrete way—make this or that policy different, have this ruler, that cabinet minister, etcetera, but beyond that," Cezal shrugged, "I don't think most people are aware of their own cultural baggage enough to know what kind of change they want. So when you get to *true* change, such as that which the rich man tried to establish, it becomes very messy and often leaves people feeling uncomfortable."

Zamen looked at him with a smile spread across his face. "Well, well, now you're starting to sound like an ideologue, eh Cezal?" He playfully nudged Cezal's shin under the table with his foot. At Cezal's lack of concrete response, he added, "Well, what do you say to *that*?"

Cezal gave a small smile. "Well, I guess you must be rubbing off on me."

* * *

A disoriented man who introduced himself as Patzal wandered into the cabin one afternoon while Cezal was alone. The autumn sun shone into the cabin uncomfortably, casting its light in an abrasive manner. Patzal seated himself on the edge of the bed, near the door, and looked into Cezal, squinting his eyes dramatically in the process.

"I do not like the people here." He leaned in, his arms tightly at his side. "You're not like the other people on the train, are you?"

"No," Cezal replied hesitantly, trying to predict what response Patzal was looking for. At the same time, he tried to seem nonchalant while making sure Patzal wouldn't get too close to his suitcase with his valuables.

"Mm," Patzal said gravely. "The people here are morally bankrupt. They don't care for others. They are evil. Evil." His eyes gleamed with sublime intensity as he babbled on, seeming to have multiple conversations at once.

"How do I know this? I have seen them. I have lived here. They are horrible. They are a stain. A stain. A stain that must be cleaned." He paused and raised an eyebrow in a knowing way, looking as though through Cezal.

"How do I know they are a stain? Because they view other types of people as a stain. Do you see what I mean? You see in others what you yourself are. They are stains. But who will clean it up?" Suddenly he focused his eyes and looked sharply into Cezal's.

"Will you?" Patzal asked. "I don't think you will." He shook his head vigorously.

"No, *I* must do it," he replied to himself.

"Come closer, my friend. You don't want them to hear you," he said.

"They don't want me here. I see through them, and they don't like that."

"Yes, I do. That is why all the other people on the train avoid me and why *my* ticket keeps getting checked. They'll throw me out as soon as it expires."

"I'll hide, though. I know how to hide." His eyes darted to all the corners of the cabin.

"Ha, but soon I'll make *them* hide."

"Where is my sandwich. Someone ate my sandwich."

Cezal interjected, "I don't kn—"

"Look at that guy over there." Cezal looked out through the open door into the cabin opposite them. A man was reading a book. "Look at his face—the gluttonous pig. The fat is practically dripping off his body. He must have taken it."

Patzal leaped up and stomped over to him.

"Hey you! Where's my sandwich? Don't lie to me." The man looked at him, eyes wide.

"I thought he had it. He *did* have it. Before he shoved it down his engorged pipe. This is what I mean. That is how they see me."

"Give me my sandwich!"

"I am the stain to them."

"The stain."

"*Daddy, why is that man dirty?*"

"Because, my boy, he is a stain. That is all he can be. Pity him—he'll be dead soon enough"

"*You're so kind and strong, Daddy.*"

"Please son, you stroke my ego in a dangerous way."

"where is my sandwich?" he yelled again.

Cezal snapped out of his trance and decided to quickly close the door on Patzal. It seemed that the man in the other cabin was getting up to do the same.

"Oh, you're just like them," Patzal yelled through the now-closed door.

* * *

The next day, in the dining car, there was something of a skirmish happening between a drunk and three police officers. It wasn't an unusual occurrence to see the men get too drunk and aggressive. Really, it's for handling such people that the train police were mostly there. That, and to make sure those who don't have tickets get off at the next stop. After some shouting and a couple of harsh words exchanged, the police officers were able to subdue the drunk. They led him to the back, and Cezal recognized it was Patzal, though Patzal didn't seem to notice Cezal.

The third officer, the one who looked the youngest, stayed back, presumably to make sure it was known there would be no tolerance of aggressive drunkenness. Whether he was doing this as a show of power or as an attempt to reassure the other passengers that things were in control was unclear. As he sauntered in Cezal's direction, he saw his nice sandwich and bottle of wine Cezal had bought from a few towns back.

"You mind if I sit for a while?" he asked, unassumingly enough. Cezal was midchew, so he gestured for him to sit on the other side of the table.

"Care for some wine?" Cezal asked. The officer tugged the sleeve of his uniform up a bit and checked his watch.

"Sure, why not," he replied.

"How old are you? You can't be older than twenty," said Cezal. The officer chuckled a bit and gave a slight smile.

"I'm older than I look. Turned twenty-five last month."

Cezal nodded.

"Well," he replied, raising his glass, "cheers to twenty-five, eh?"

The officer nodded his head a bit in turn. "Cheers."

"So what happens to the people you detain?" Cezal asked. "I almost never see them again. Do you just kick them out at the next stop?"

The young officer gave a knowing smile. "Well, it depends on who's shift leader that day. Often, once the ruffian is subdued, if necessary, we give them more alcohol until they're completely passed out, then we strip their clothes and check for valuables. If it's dark, we'll throw him out of the train then and there. Most of the men on this train have no one who would miss them anyways—especially so for almost all the alcoholics. If anything, by dumping them, we're doing their families a favor."

This guy seemed the type to talk too much and to value his opinions more than he likely should, so Cezal stayed silent and waited for him to continue, regretting his over-friendliness and having offered wine. *Where was Zamen when you needed him?* He continued eating his sandwich, resolving simply to nod or grunt at the appropriate times for the officer's story.

"You know, I came from a small town way out," the officer continued. "It was an hour away by horse to even the first paved road, and then three more hours before you could get to the nearest train stop. Most of the men there were loggers. They'd work for a few weeks at a time and then come home for a few days, bringing the money to their families before going out, usually less than a week later, back into the forest. In my village, at least, other than the extra income the men brought, they were largely an unwelcome presence. Broken souls, most of them were."

The policeman shook his head and took a gulp of wine.

"I grew up in such an environment and hated it. I resolved that wouldn't be me, so as soon as I got old enough, I left. I came to the railroad to be a police officer. I remember, as a kid, riding with my mom on the train, they were the ones who brought order. They were the ones who commanded respect—and that's a difficult thing to get nowadays," he added, nodding as he did. "And, the pay isn't half bad if you consider the tips. Anyhow, my point here is that most of these drunks we throw off are better off dead in a ditch than at home." He sighed, got up, and made a cursory survey of the car before getting seated again. "Just to be clear," he said matter-of-factly and with a hint of sensitive reassurance, "*you're* the one who asked what we do. I'm giving you this backstory for your sake, not mine."

Cezal leaned back slightly.

"I have no need to try and push away the guilt that usually comes with killing someone else. I don't value human lives enough to have a guilty conscience." He gave a small chuckle after seeing the expression on Cezal's face. "Why tell you this in the first place? I can tell that you're the kind of person who can keep a secret. You're also the kind of person who doesn't get outraged. That's why I like you—I've seen how you are. And, I suppose everyone likes to talk about themselves, even more so after splitting some wine. Thank you for the glass, by the way."

Cezal sat there, looking at him, rather unsure of what to say but trying to seem unfazed. He started to reply when—

"Well, I have to get back to work. But I'd close your mouth before a bug gets sucked in." The officer chuckled. Then, with a sigh, he pushed himself to a standing position, gave Cezal a sturdy clap on the back, and continued walking down the train. "Let me know if anyone gives you trouble," he said on the way out.

7

———

Another night, later that week, while Cezal was again having his dinner alone, Bekochan entered the dining car and headed toward the lone diner, his downtrodden air following him. He looked over at Cezal with a feeble smile that seemed to ask permission to come over. Cezal smiled back, by this time, rather wary of strange people simply coming to sit with him—something that seemed to be happening quite a bit lately. He did his best, however, to be accommodating to the bereaved figure now before him.

"I'd like to apologize for my behavior the other night," Bekochan began. "I was quite out-of-sorts then. Thank you for the coffee and water. Have you already eaten, or?"

"Yes, I've eaten—"

"Oh, well, in that case," he offered quickly, "please, let me get you a cup of coffee at least."

Cezal gave a kind smile. "That would be nice. Thank you."

Bekochan got up hurriedly, wringing his hands lightly as he walked over to the dispensers. Cezal thought of how long he really wanted this conversation to last. Perhaps he would make it short—drink the cup in a timely manner and make his excuses. Bekochan, of course, would understand.

Outside, the darkness crept by, and the train felt steeped in nature and isolation, likely the only hint of humanity for thousands of kilometers in any direction. The other patrons kept on eating, the dining car almost as though an other-worldly capsule, venturing through the vast unknown. The senior special, which always included a salad somehow, had ended a few hours ago. Now, if you wanted food, you had to buy it at the counter, off of an itemized menu. By the looks of it, it was the son of the chef in the esteemed position to be vendor-of-late-night-snacks. He gave off an air of apathy that one could have perhaps most succinctly described as *palpable*. No doubt he wished he were spending his youth not on a train in the middle-of-nowhere ladling out thin soup and stale bread, but rather with people his own age doing whatever it is they do. And what is it again that people his age do? Suddenly, Bekochan returned, forcing Cezal out of his contemplation.

"Here you are." Bekochan placed both cups down, having brought them over, holding them by the lip. "I apologize, this is really quite embarrassing, but could you remind me of your name?" he asked as he sat down.

Cezal watched his impromptu companion take his hands off the cups. "Oh, it's quite fine. I'm Cezal."

"Ah, well, nice to meet you then." Bekochan let out a sigh and stared out the window, his hands clasping the cup in a dainty fashion. It seemed as though he were trying to look out at the landscape, but in the night only the interior of the train was visible. Cezal tried to follow what he saw but found instead just Bekochan's empty reflection and worn clothes, themselves in need of more than a few patches and likely a good wash.

"I'm from the far north," began Bekochan abruptly, still looking out the window. "And there, in the summer, the sun stays up for many hours of the day—at times never dipping below the horizon for more than an hour or so. My dad used to tell me stories about the sun, saying that in the olden days, on the summer solstice, the villagers would all have a wonderful festival with much merriment for all. On this day, the sun is said to have descended from the sky to come to join the people at their midsummer festival. It would bring warm milk and strawberry juice for the children and sacks of oats and chicken eggs for the adults. In turn, the people would share their food and art with the sun and enjoy catching up and sharing the stories of what happened in the past year—details of the strange travelers who wandered through town, the children who were born, those who had died, the next-door neighbor's crazy obsession with trying to grow squash, how the Altjenins' oldest son had run off to the big city in the south in order to be a toy crafter. Things like that."

Cezal smiled warmly. "It sounds like it was a wonderful time."

Bekochan smiled back and nodded. "Yes, it certainly was. They would essentially tell the sun all the gossip that such towns live off of. And to these stories, the sun would laugh, give consolation, or be a shoulder upon which to cry. The village people all loved it for that. That day, according to my father, was always a perfect one. And as it wore on, the celebration would get increasingly merry, and eventually, they would all build a bonfire and do dances. At first, they did the traditional ones the oldest generation all learned, followed by the dances of the adults, and then the children until it was simply a time of festivity and the villagers would play their drums and string instruments late into the day. They all danced with such joy, the sun always taking much part too. Then, when it came to be noon of the following day, the summer sun would again smile warmly at all the people and thank them for their kind hospitality and tell them, alas, it was time to go, but that it was such a nice celebration and it was very glad to have shared that time with everyone. 'Until next year,' it would say, and then go back up again." Bekochan gave a little smile after finishing his story, staring ever still into the darkness outside.

Cezal smiled a bit himself and looked down for a second. "That's a nice story, Bekochan. What made you think of it?"

He looked over and shrugged his shoulders a bit, seeming a bit higher in spirits in the process. "Oh, it's just a pleasant story," he said, staring more at Cezal's cup than at Cezal. "When it gets to be later in autumn, and the sun starts setting noticeably earlier, it always comes to mind. We're a lot further south here. My dad and I, we lived near as north as you could go, really. Where we are now, and where the train's headed, I don't think there's ever less than four hours of darkness, even in the summer. It's funny in that way. Maybe there's something to be said for extremes. I suppose they kind of work together."

Cezal looked at Bekochan, and for a second, they locked eyes. "I suppose so, don't they."

They sat like that for some time more until many of the guests were gone. The train continued to clack as ever, and the outside world kept going imperceptibly by, elegantly cloaked by the night. Cezal took to simply watching the train and feeling its rhythm as they both sipped away. Eventually, he got up and bid Bekochan goodbye.

"Thank you," Bekochan said. "It's been nice."

Cezal nodded his head and smiled. "Yes, it has been."

* * *

"Have you given more thought to what you want to do once you get to Sectohal? Do you even know what town you'll get off at?" Zamen asked the next morning as he changed from his pajamas to his daytime clothes. The sun at this time was filtering in nicely and was unseasonably warm. Somehow, it felt rather more intense than it had the previous week. Now, they were heading out of the more steppelike region, and there came to be more and more trees, again pine, though aspen groves were not entirely uncommon either.

Cezal looked up from his book he was reading while still lying in bed and put it down, resting it on the table between them and shifting so he was on his side and resting on his elbow. He shook his head a bit. "To be honest, I haven't really given it all that much thought. My ticket is for the regional capital, Briedavga. I made it for there just because it's the only sizable city in the region, so they're bound to have jobs for me, and besides, I have enough saved up to keep me for some time, so I'm in no particular rush."

"And what do you see yourself doing there?" Zamen asked, staring out the window.

"Well, I supposed I always just considered I'd try to get a job relating to banking. Otherwise, I don't know. Get a hotel room for a while, as I look for someplace to lodge for a longer stretch. Perhaps I'll find an upper-story hovel-like room. The kind where the bathroom is a broom closet if you're lucky and the sink itself is in the same room as everything else, sticking out like a sore thumb on a poorly plastered wall with a single window looking out onto the city."

"Hm, well, it certainly sounds like you have quite the romanticized image of what it will be like."

"Well, I suppose so," Cezal replied, rather more back to earth by now.

"And what will you do when it's not as nice as you imagine it will be?"

Cezal shook his head. "Well, I don't know. I know the wonder of it all will wear off in not too long. I'll find ways to get myself engaged with the community. Who knows? Perhaps I'll settle down there. Yes, it'll be different, and I'll be marked the outsider, but it will be something new. I'm sure I needn't justify to you my ability to handle myself."

"No, no, of course not," replied Zamen while he looked out the window. "It's only that, well, I know *my* plan is rather out there, but even to me, your plan strikes me as rather directionless and unimaginative."

"Oh?" Cezal replied nonchalantly, by now used to the frankness with which Zamen spoke. "Well, perhaps so. You're the type to seek out an exciting life. I'm much more easily contented."

Zamen nodded softly and in a drawn-out fashion. "Yes, that may be so, but I think it would still be good to look at it not simply as a question of 'what will I do?' but rather as a matter of 'what do I want to get out of what I do?' For the first time in a long while, you will have no one who knows anything about you, and you won't be in some small, claustrophobic village out in the desert." Zamen waved his hands out as though shooing away a bird as he said that last phrase. "Briedavga's a sizable place. It's a real fresh start you'll have there."

Cezal paused for a bit. "Yes, well, I suppose you have a point. But I'm also rather okay with who I am. I feel no need for reinvention."

Zamen pushed his lips out and shrugged his signature way, and continued looking out the window. "I suppose there's nothing wrong with that, so long as you really want what you already have, and it's not that you're just comfortable as you are. Because there's really nothing to be gained from comfort."

"What are you suggesting, Zamen?"

"I wonder if perhaps you haven't questioned yourself that much—really asked yourself, 'Why do I believe what I do?' I hope you take no offense to it. I certainly don't mean to come off as some prick who thinks he knows more than he does. I only bring it up because I've seen a lot of people who haven't really questioned themselves all that much or all that fully. Because of their lack of introspection, those people see walls where there are none. They have not truly questioned the validity of their beliefs and what their priorities are. Life, Cezal, is just a game, and the barriers of society are merely unspoken rules to the game that we've managed to all more or less accept as how it is and our lot in life. By this, I don't mean to suggest that you stick it to the man or anything like that. There's nothing to prove to anyone, of course. It's simply a matter of being fully honest and sincere with yourself." He sighed a bit and nodded. "Oh, sincerity—now *there's* an undervalued trait."

Cezal absorbed what he said and made a note to consider it later. "You make some good points, Zamen, but I must say, it sounds rather ironic to hear that *you* value sincerity so much."

Zamen looked over at him. "How so?"

"Well, I mean, trying to be an ideologue and all—it involves being able to manipulate and charm, wouldn't you say? There can't be too much sincerity in that."

Zamen stared out the window for a moment, and in that time, appeared to be carefully considering his words. The rolling hills and the pine trees flowed by.

"I see where you're coming from. And there is perhaps a level of truth to that," he sighed. "But I am speaking of a different kind of sincerity—a different kind of authenticity. The kind of authenticity that doesn't mean being transparent in one's actions, but rather, transparent in intentions." He shifted how he sat and now faced his companion squarely. "As a parent, you may see your child is doing something not good for them, but that they nonetheless enjoy. Perhaps they are wasting too much time sitting around as a shut-in reading valueless books, not engaging enough with the world. Yes, it is more comfortable for them to be in their room doing whatever they occupy themself with, but it is not good for the long-term development of the child. If they were older, you could level with them. You might say that you think what they are doing is self-destructive and unhelpful in the long run. In turn, they would consider your words, look at their life and ask themself critically if what you say is true."

"Do you really think would be a very effective strategy?" Cezal asked.

Zamen leaned in casually and nodded. "Assuming they're wise enough and capable enough of self-introspection, then yes, they would change their habits accordingly. But consider the case of a young child—one who sees only the instant enjoyment they get out of such unproductive activities. As a parent, you know it is a waste of breath to level with your young child the same way you would your adult child." He raised his palm in his explanatory way. "So you would come up with different ways of trying to reach them. Perhaps you would take them to various social engagements or, if you yourself weren't particularly skilled in the art of tactfulness, perhaps you would lecture or even belittle them. That, of course, would be rather unproductive and would speak to your own need for more self-cultivation, but I digress. In any case, you wouldn't be completely transparent with your child. Nor would you likely say to them, 'I am worried about you.' Because that would just make them feel bad about themself, as though there were something wrong with them. It is the same in the case for an ideologue, except we are like parents to society as a whole. It is thus our job to have the wisdom to perceive the people properly and understand how to reach them. Oftentimes, that means doing differently than we say." He shrugged.

Cezal made a sign to show he was considering what Zamen said, and they both sat in silence for a while.

"I apologize if I'm rambling," Zamen began a few moments later. "At this point, I'm just thinking out loud… I think people make themselves out to be too much. We're just a complex system in the end, no different than a machine in that sense. It may feel denigrating to hear it that way, but in the end, how *are* we different than a machine? Huh? What is this *essence* of a human being I hear so often talked about? There's nothing so special or irreplicable. What then is the secret to a fulfilling life? That is an important question to which an ideologue must appear to know the answer. People look for this or that simple answer, but really, just like any complex system, there are so many elements that go into it. It is supported by many *healthy factors*, if you will, that all mesh together and add up to a content person. This is why it is said people have to *cultivate* themselves and their lives. It is a long process. Just as we have economic analysts who give counsel on policy, and if all the factors of the economy work well, then, perhaps five or ten years later, we begin to see a healthy economy—that's how humans are too. It takes time to see results, and progress will be messy."

Cezal tilted his head to the side. "I don't know, Zamen. I don't think it's proper to say we're just *machines*. There may be nothing essential to a human, but that doesn't mean we can just be reduced to finite states."

Zamen stared blankly at him for a moment. "Well, perhaps so. But you understand my metaphor, no?"

Cezal nodded hesitantly. "Yes, I suppose so."

"Well, so then you see how in this day and age, that is precisely the job of an ideologue. We must look at society and diagnose it with such and such malady and prescribe some treatment or another. And that, too, is why those who expect a society to be run as one would a business are sorely misguided. A government should be run as a family. Make no mistake. I do not say this out of some deep love for humanity. I say it because it is pragmatic. A company is there to make profits. That is its job. A government is not there to make profits. It is there to foster a healthy society.

"There is a certain overbearing moral arrogance to those who staunchly view the world in such black-and-white terms. 'The world is a jungle,' they say, patting themselves on the back for their paltry self-asceticism. Bah! If only they knew how good they have it and how foolish it is to slander the good fortune that has befallen them! But I digress, the ideologue must be the parent, and those whom the ideologue serves are the children. We see the complexities of humans and their societies and perceive what needs to change in order to make it better. Just as a parent would, we guide society down the right path. This is what gives ideologues our power and influence. We perceive the times and the people and act accordingly. There's little more to it, really."

* * *

The following morning, Cezal got a late start. With the days being shorter, he found himself with less energy and more easily tired. On this morning, he awoke with the sunlight streaming in, beautiful in a midautumn way—a certain golden tinge about it. He simply laid in bed for a while, Zamen having gotten up before dawn, likely off to the common room to read or to someone else's cabin to talk. By Cezal's supine view, he could only see the occasional tops of the trees they passed. The terrain was getting rockier, with rolling hills, the occasional one even looking more like a small mountain than anything else. There was more water now too, and they passed streams and lakes far more frequently.

"We've passed the continental divide," Zamen had announced one day not too long ago while they were both reading quietly. "Now, all the rivers you see head north." *To the end of the continent,* thought Cezal, *to the barren, desolate north.* It was a strange thought to him that you could have gone on the river and simply floated, and it would bring you to the end of the world, where the wind whipped and nothing could grow. Like portals to another life, they flowed.

This day was overcast, though not in the blanketed overcast way that is most common at that time of the year. Rather it was a thinner layer that covered the sky, and one could make out individual clouds below. Cezal took to simply looking at them, lulled by the rhythmic clacking of the train, as he drifted in and out of lucidity, reflecting on the last day's conversations.

After a while, he grew hungry enough he finally got out of bed, still somewhat groggy. He checked his pocket watch—nearly noon. He put on some straw slippers and, in his ragamuffin pajamas, stepped out to the hall to fetch some coffee, cheese, and bread. He found himself paying more attention to the carpet as he walked. So full of stains it was, the patterned maroon and formerly dandelion yellow was contrasting with his slippers and black socks. He wondered whose idea it was to put carpet in a practically third-rate train.

Suddenly, a door slid open a few cabins back, and Zamen called out, "Cezal!… Cezal!" He turned around. "Yes, good morning to you. Bring us a couple of cups of coffee and some pastries, then come join us, would you?"

Cezal looked at him, somewhat phased, before uttering some words in the affirmative and going to the canteen. They were out of pastries and bread and cheese, so there was only the lukewarm coffee leftover from earlier that morning.

He walked back, curious as to whom Zamen was with, and slid open the door.

"Good morning, Cezal!" greeted Zamen in his charming way. "Thank you for bringing the coffee. Here," he gestured with his arms, "come sit. I was just talking with Alja, who is an artist—principally a painter if I'm not mistaken?" He looked over to her as he said this, and she nodded in the affirmative. "And she just so happens to be going to Sectohal as well. Anyhow, we've just been talking for a little while now, and I thought you'd like to meet her. This is Cezal, by the way," Zamen added as he gestured toward him. Cezal smiled as best he could in his grogginess and introduced himself as he sat down.

"So," she began, "Zamen told me about your plans. I've been to Briedavga. It's probably the only place in the region that can be considered a true city. The rest is mostly just forest and small settlements here and there."

"Yes," said Zamen. "Even here, it feels rather like we're at the edge of the world. I can't remember the last time we even saw a village."

"Yes, well," explained Alja, "where we are now could perhaps be considered even more sparsely populated. The region we're in gets far colder, and the land is either rocky or boglike, which of course doesn't lend itself too well to farming. But we still have some time before we get to Sectohal. There, at least, we'll come to some small towns once or twice."

They continued talking for some time, getting through standard introductions and things of that nature, going on for at least a couple of hours more, through lunch. In the process, they went through Zamen's backstory, with him giving a light version of his plans for Kevelga.

Alja, too, began talking about herself and why she was heading to Sectohal. "I grew up in a very rural area. My maternal grandfather was a farmer. He worked the fields, growing mostly wheat, kale, and black tomatoes. The whole family lived there for a while, but when I was five or six, we moved maybe a half-day away by horse to a cabin out in the woods. My father was never the type to like the farm life, so we moved where he could better be a fur trapper. Yes, we all quite resented him for that! Taking us out of everything we knew just so he could more easily hunt sable. If I'm being honest, it doesn't make much sense to have gone there—as a frontiersman, you really weren't home much anyway, but anyhow, that was the reason given to me for our having relocated. I had two brothers and one sister, all of whom were at least ten years older than me, so they had all already moved to the big city, some two days by train. Though, of course, we didn't have a train then, so it was a little longer than a week to get back and forth. As you can imagine, they weren't a big fixture in my life."

"What made you leave?" Cezal asked.

"Well, I never particularly liked it there. It was really a rather lonely existence. I pleaded for my family to send me to live with one of my older siblings. It didn't matter particularly whom, as long as I could stay in Briedavga. Once I turned sixteen, they capitulated and let me live with my older sister in her apartment with her husband. I'm sure it's not interesting to hear my entire life story, but to tell it in short, I lived there a few years while I worked in a tannery. The fumes were horrible, and it did no good for my health. My sister saw this and tried to get me to go back to my family, but when I refused, she decided to send me to Nesge, in the West, because at least there were far more people, far more jobs, and much more money. And so I went and never looked back.

"That's where I started my career as an artist. For a while, I worked in a rather high-end café, serving the many posh people who happened by. It was nice—no horrible fumes, and it gave one time and space to think. I started painting in my spare time, and by virtue of having often served the well-connected, I was able to quickly get my art out into the world and popular enough that I only had to work part-time. Eventually, I simply continued at the café because I enjoyed the work. Ah, but recently I've felt rather… stale, and I thought, after nearly twenty years living in the same city—the same shabby apartment even—it would do me some good to revisit my past. Of course, my parents are dead now, and the cabin has simply been left to disrepair for all I know. But I'll find it, or at least what's left of it. Who knows how long I will stay. I've yet to send a message to my older sister to let her know I'll be back. We never saw each other in the time I've been gone."

"Oh, I see," Cezal said, leaning back. "Yes, that is quite a while."

She nodded. "We write every once in a while, but communication is rather sparse. It is understandable, though—we really have little space in each other's lives." She shrugged and took a sip of coffee. "And you, Cezal. Do you have any siblings?"

"Oh no—for the longest time, it was just my mother and me. We lived in our tight-knit little town, and really that's all I've known. This is the most I've ever traveled."

"Ah, well then, this must all be rather exciting," she added as she smiled.

He smiled back and nodded politely. "And what kind of art is it that you do—just paintings?" he asked.

"Mostly so, yes. I'm quite fond of the post-expressionists—I consider my work to be more or less of the same movement."

At this point, Zamen, who had been sitting this whole time quietly, simply listening, decided to involve himself again. So she and Zamen got into a discussion about his ideology, and Cezal, still not quite having woken up as much as one would have hoped, wasn't particularly in the mood to hear him rehash what they had already talked about many times before in their own cabin.

He noted as well that whenever Zamen was talking on a subject Cezal had already talked about with him, he had the rather insufferable tendency to steer the conversation to the same talking points they'd had the first time. He'd overheard other conversations that Zamen had with people. They flowed more organically and had original conversation, and Cezal could only imagine this was some sort of pettily artful power play. When Cezal was around, it always felt like Zamen was having the same conversation. The experience was simply bizarre for him, especially since it did seem that Zamen was rather skillful at it.

Had Cezal not been paying attention, it wouldn't have felt like an artificial or one-sided conversation. What this said about Zamen, Cezal really didn't know. It was just weird, and he didn't have the energy to condemn him over such an obscure tendency. In the meantime, the day was slipping into late-afternoon, and Cezal looked out the window, a cup of hot water in hand, and watched as the sun dipped lower and lower, casting itself through the trees, creating quite a dramatic effect of light and shadow flowing through the cabin. Oh, what a time to be alive.

* * *

In the following days, Zamen took to sitting, thinking, and writing more than he had before. There hadn't been any late-night gatherings for at least a week now. Nor was he going out and talking with other passengers, with the exception of when his fellow 'rapscallions,' as Zamen termed them, would come to the cabin themselves to socialize.

On one afternoon, while the evening light was streaming in, Zamen was simply lying in bed, fully clothed, with his legs stretched out, his hands clasped on his chest. He stared singularly at the black, lacquered ceiling. The clacking of the train was the only sound he heard, punctuated by the odd slight bump from one side to another as the rail curved. The ideologue's taught skin made the crinkles on his face from furrowing his eyebrows or moving his mouth, as though he were having a closed-lipped conversation, seem even more stark and dramatic.

Cezal himself was leisurely reading a book he had bought a few towns back and enjoyed a cup of tea at the table. In boredom, he put down his book. "What are you thinking about, Zamen?" he asked when it looked from his face he had come to a lull in thought.

Zamen, somewhat startled, looked quickly to Cezal with wide eyes. "Oh, well, I'm just thinking. I get off the train the morning after tomorrow, and, well, it's certainly starting to seem more real now. Of course, I'll mostly just be making myself acquainted with the town at first, but this will be rather a new life for me. There'll be no going back once I leave," he trailed off. "Well, I suppose there is, but I need to think there's no going back so that when I really cross the Rubicon, it will feel as though a river like any other... But as well, and what is perhaps weighing down on my mind more, is thinking about the ideology.

"I have researched this town extensively. I know its history, its almanac from the last two decades, its culture, its everything really. I know it as well as one possibly could from print materials. But of course, it's one thing to know and another to experience and apply. And I suppose as well, I'm thinking of the longevity of the ideology. It needs to be able to exist independently of myself after enough time. Otherwise, it will be considered rather weak—no better than a cult of personality, if that even. I am considering how necessary it is to include a concept that will likely manifest to have my ideology develop the trappings of an intrinsic ideology while remaining an extrinsic ideology at its core. It is a risk..." He rolled over to face Cezal, placing his hand pensively over his mouth. "I suppose that makes me rather a hypocrite then, eh?"

Cezal raised his eyebrows and his left palm off the table. "Well, I suppose that could be said. But, and this sounds like something I feel like you yourself would say, it doesn't matter if *you* are hypocritical—what matters is the prolongation of the ideology."

Zamen smiled a bit. "Yes, that is something I would say. And I think you're right. It may reflect somewhat poorly on me, but one must keep in mind that the ideology is always bigger than the ideologue."

There was a lull, and Zamen rolled over again onto his back.

"What kind of changes are you thinking of?" Cezal asked.

Zamen stared wide-eyed at the ceiling. "I'm not quite sure. It's difficult to predict the way that ideology will manifest itself in the real world. You can, of course, have some concept or value or whatever that you include in the theory of your ideology, but then the people take it, and, as with anything, it will evolve and manifest itself in unpredictable ways. It is, by this nature, not a science but rather an exercise in the art of perception. I suppose I likely won't make a certain decision until I've been there for some time, but suffice it to say, I think I'll need to add in the concept of debt."

Cezal knit his eyebrows, "Debt? What do you mean by debt? Surely you don't mean monetary debt."

Zamen gave a strong expression, "Oh no, no, I haven't gone that far, Cezal." And he gave a light chuckle. "And even so, the concept of money is a rather poor means of strengthening an ideology, especially a fledgling one. It's often more of an end in itself, observed only in well-established ideologies that are more engrained in the culture in which it operates. No, this debt is of a different kind. Debt, in general, is really a very powerful and, if you're not careful, insidious concept. The thing with debt is that it's tied so closely with guilt and obligation, but you can impose it almost anywhere. It isn't that difficult, really, to make people feel as though by virtue of their existence, they have a heavy debt. Such has been done throughout history time and time again.

"To what or whom your debt is owed—that matters far less. It's about the debt itself and whether or not it can be paid off. I've considered for my ideology if there should be a debt to society, a debt to a higher power, or even a debt to existence itself." He shook his head tightly. "The closer you get to a fundamental aspect of what it means to exist as a human in that culture, the more volatile the manifestations of the concept. With this logic, the riskiest, though potentially most gripping concept I can go with, is debt to existence itself," he sighed. "Ah, but again, that's the problem. Yes, debt can make an ideology take a stronger hold and make it spread even better, but as the ideology changes, if it goes in a bad direction, the stronger the concept of debt, the harder it would be for an ideologue to come in and correct it. Well," he turned to Cezal again, "I suppose at this point, I'm just thinking out loud. But you see what I'm considering here."

Cezal nodded pensively. "What makes you think your ideology won't be strong enough without debt?"

Zamen put up his arms again in the slightly exasperated way he always did when explaining things. "Well, it could survive on its own without debt, but, to put it in other terms, I suppose you can think of ideology in this case as clay. An ideologue can mold it however they want, and, in the beginning, this can be done with relative ease, depending, of course, on what the preexisting ideology there already is. They may be successful in shaping it in the way they want, and it may work symbiotically with the society it exists in. But the problem is that if it's so malleable, it's easy for other people, or even unpredictable societal forces, to come in and mash it in a way that's no good. Debt is like a strong fire, fixing the clay into a specific shape. It makes it such that someone else couldn't so easily mess it up, or, in the case of religion, for example, it makes it so that in hard times, people have an easier time keeping hope and faith. It is a difficult balance that must be found. I think at least to some degree, I must make there be debt, otherwise, someone else will just add the concept themself down the line, and likely not to my liking."

"That's an interesting idea," Cezal said. He took to thinking about it for a while, and so for that time, they were both simply staring into space in a dark room, the muffled sound of conversation next door. Eventually, Cezal turned a side lamp on and went back to reading his book. This must have gone on for at least a half-an-hour or so.

"I think I'll make it a debt to a perfect society," Zamen said, his voice cutting through the hazy mood of the room.

"Oh?"

"Yes," he affirmed. "That's my best course of action, to make sure that the ideology, even if it changes ostensibly, keeps its ultimate end at heart. After all, it's for a better society that I'm even creating this ideology in the first place. In this case, the risk lies in what the people come to define a better society as, but that's certainly more manageable than something like debt for existence."

"So how will you add this kind of debt?" Cezal asked.

"Well," began Zamen, "it will depend. Put simply, it's largely just a matter of framing the ideology such that it becomes clear it is important to work toward having a perfect society, and that we must all work together to create it. It is just about the extent to which one reinforces this principle. And even then, it's a question of how people will interpret it. The biggest question here is what exactly *is* a perfect society? I will say a perfect society is one that cultivates value to the highest possible degree. The individual pursuit for happiness, as it seems to so often be put, isn't pointed enough. People are, on average, rather poor at cultivating a happy life and are too easily swayed by their momentary fancy that to simply have such freedom would be rather... unwieldy."

"But then how do you define value?" Cezal asked.

Zamen smiled, appearing to be impressed by the question, and sat up, leaning forward on both arms on the bed. "Ah yes, that's a more difficult question. It relies, however, on some form of social cohesion. People need something outside of themselves to live for in order to cultivate meaningful lives. Any value created would thus have something to do with that... Perhaps for the sake of ease and for cultivating the proper image in people's minds, I will use the allegory of a perfect town—utopian, really. The idea of this town is what people should devote their lives to. Once it is complete, the town shall be perfect, and all who live there will be happy and satisfied."

"I feel that you've perhaps lost your point, Zamen, don't you think? How could such a town ever actually exist?" Cezal asked.

At that, Zamen gave a knowing smile and tilted his head to the side. "Ah yes, how *could* such a town ever exist? The answer is simple—it never could, and that's why it's so wonderful. People don't actually like achieving their goals—not *really*. They like comfort, and perhaps more importantly, they like to believe in something."

"Yes, but in this case, that something to believe in could never exist," Cezal replied.

"Of course, but that's why it works because in working and believing so sincerely in something—to do so means that you hold the conception of it in full. If that something is a thing that could never exist, then even better—you can make the unreal, well, real. Why do you think the iconoclasts cared so much about the destruction of religious icons?"

Cezal tilted his head. "I'm afraid I've lost your point, Zamen."

He nodded. "I'll tell you why. It's because once they saw their deities in physical form, they had to ask themselves, 'Is this all there is? Is this whom I devote my life to? Perhaps these statues aren't representing anything at all—perhaps there's nothing at all to even be represented.' And thus is the crux of the problem—you can more fully believe in something when there's nothing that exists to represent it; when you know it never *can* exist."

Cezal inhaled through his teeth and tilted his head to the side. "I suppose I see your point now, Zamen, but that's exactly the thing—there never will be the payoff of getting the utopian society."

Zamen gave a tight smile. "Once again, Cezal, the payoff exists in the belief itself."

"Won't you then be trying to get people to live for a time they will never really live in?" Cezal asked.

"I suppose you could think of it in such a way, but it doesn't need to be so."

"Yes, but don't you think it's important to base oneself in reality—to be pragmatic about the world."

Zamen squinted his eyes almost in disbelief. "But Cezal, I *am* being pragmatic—I'm simply honest about human nature."

Cezal shook his head lightly. "I don't think so, Zamen."

Zamen leaned forward over the table to Cezal and took a drawn-out sigh of restraint. "Luckily, Cezal, you needn't." And he leaned back again.

Cezal dropped the subject and went back to reading, though he found it rather unbecoming for someone who was trying to be such a person-of-the-people to be so easily put on edge in a stressful situation.

Zamen lay back down. The train continued as it always did, and the mood of the night came through the curtained windows. The muted lights attached to the table were all that lit the room. From the outside, the forest was silent but, of course, for the train, which rushed through, the lights from the cabins glowing through the trees and the cold, alpine air. Once the train passed, all the animals in the forest, many preparing to go into hibernation, held their collective breath, and it would be silent in the forest until after enough time passed and the normal nocturnal noises resumed.

Zamen sat upright and broke the relative silence. "It is the right decision, Cezal. People do not care for their own happiness—they wish only to strive for it."

"Well," Cezal replied, "I don't know if you can categorically assert that."

Zamen gave a tight smile and opened his mouth a second before speaking. "I don't *need* to categorically assert it. The ideologue imposes the narrative unto the people, and thus the people become what the ideologue proclaims unto them. Here, I am saying that the people don't actually want happiness—they want only to strive for it. As such, I will make it so."

"I don't know, Zamen," Cezal replied unhesitatingly. "You speak like someone who thinks he knows things he doesn't."

"And if I do?" replied Zamen, his eyebrow raising.

"Well, don't you think that discredits a lot of what you say and think?"

"You'll have to forgive me, Cezal, if I start to become somewhat short with you. But it's certainly understandable not to like to have the validity of what one stands for be questioned.

I do not say what I say for your sake. You do not know me." Zamen began to stand up but stopped himself and sat back down, emoting instead with his arms and hands. "If you wish to write me off, then so be it. Do not, however, think you can make me question myself. I am not infallible. I know this very well. But I do not speak flippantly about *anything*. It may appear so to you, but this is because to most people, being familiar makes one seem more trustworthy—more real. I suppose I have misjudged you and how you would interpret the seeming candidness with which I speak. But I assure you, dear Cezal, there is not a single thing I say that is uncalculated."

Cezal leaned back, trying to contain his resurfacing odium.

"I would have thought this possibility would have crossed your mind at one point or another. I have told you that there is no substance to humans—that there is only the idea we have of ourselves and the idea that others have of us. I know this quite well and have used it to my advantage. And so I know: there is no *I*. There is only the *I* that I wish you to see. As for who I tell myself I am?" He jabbed his finger into his chest fervidly. "I am a *means*. A means to an end—that is all. Nothing more and nothing less." He exhaled sharply. "You see, my intentions require me to think thusly of myself—such is how all true ideologues think. Oh, and ego. I can't forget that. That is what drives me. That is part of what makes me reveal myself to you now. And here is the thing, Cezal, here is the beauty of your little predicament: you must trust that I have good intentions. You must trust that I want good for the world. Otherwise, you should kill me right here and now." He smiled, a glint in his eye. "I know you don't have the strength to do the latter, Cezal, so I certainly hope that you believe the former."

Cezal stared at the man before him, trying to appear nonchalant and figure out what to say.

"Do you see this?" Zamen said, pointing again to his chest. "Do you see the rage? Do you see the evil? I *hope* so. It is disgust that fills me now—disgust for your existence. I know you will back down. Even now, you look at me with eyes of half-disbelief. But don't act as though you didn't see the signs."

Cezal continued looking blankly at Zamen and resisted the urge for his hands to fidget.

"My point here is that I will not be questioned by you if you expect me to back down. I know I will make mistakes, and I will misjudge, but what, oh wise Cezal, is the alternative? Shall I slink away into the shadows and wallow in self-misery for the rest of my life. I will tell you now—most of the stories I have told you of my past are false. I made them up either to make a point or to get you to see me in a certain way. But, and this is crucial, they are truths nonetheless because they may as well have happened—because *I* am the creator of myself. It is simply by chance that such stories didn't occur.

"But I digress. I will not hide in the shadows. I will not fade into existence for fear of what *you* think of me. I used to do that. I used to live for others—for the *you*. But then I saw the truth of the situation. I saw the error of my ways. I killed that self and rose from the ashes. So do not question *me* for following my intuition, for believing in what I believe in after careful analysis. I will not accept that from anyone, and I certainly will not accept that from you. Oh, Cezal," the name now seemed to have taken on a bitter taste in Zamen's mouth, "there are a thousand lives you could have lived. But, ha! You've lived this one, so you'll have to forgive me if I don't waste any more of my time entertaining your trifles."

Cezal shifted uncomfortably but still was unsure of how to respond, annoyed at himself for appearing so weak.

"I am glad that you have left your little confrontation for the end of my journey, so I will have to deal with you only one more night." He took a deep breath and seemed calmed as though suddenly satisfied. "Now go to bed. Tomorrow morning, as usual, I will wake up, and I will bring two cups of tea. I will wake you kindly, and we will have a pleasant breakfast talk. Then at my stop, at which we shall arrive at 9:12 a.m., we will bid kind farewell, and we will not talk of what has just happened. It will be pleasant. I say this for your sake. Do you not want our last encounter to be pleasant?"

Cezal gave a somewhat disgusted smile and tilted his head to the side. "Zamen, even you have to admit that it will be rather spoiled, knowing that this has all been an act."

Zamen paused for a second and looked at him single-mindedly, not particularly angry anymore, but intense, nonetheless. "Everything is an act. How many times must I tell you—there is no *I*. As such, I do not hate you any more or less than I ever did. I do not love you any more or less than I ever did. I *am* being genuine right now. When I say I have revealed myself to you, it just means I have simply revealed my intentions. Cezal, I am just a mask. So too are you. Paint it however you'd like. It doesn't change the fact that it covers nothing. If you wish to rehash what I have just said tomorrow morning, then you can. I will not deny it. I stand by what I say, especially what I just said. But I can tell you now there is little value to be found in continuing this conversation."

Cezal turned his head and gave an incredulous laugh. "Well… I suppose then we may as well be pleasant."

"Yes, that would be quite nice," Zamen replied curtly. "Now, it's nearly half-past two in the morning. You should get some sleep. Good night." He laid down again and turned his back to Cezal.

Shortly later, Cezal put his book down and turned off the light.

* * *

The next morning, the winter light came through the window in its own gentle way, with somewhat of a chill to the room—an odd combination in conjunction with the stuffiness. Cezal awoke to the sound of Zamen sliding the door open with two cups of tea in hand.

Cezal sat up and faced Zamen at the table. The steam of the cups rose more prominently than it had in times past—at least it seemed so to Cezal.

"Well, I guess this is it isn't it?" Zamen broke in, smiling a self-assured smile painted over with washed-down sorrow. "You know, it's been good talking, I have to say. It's been good." He paused. "For the sake of clarity, I have to preface my goodbye properly. We all know—once you say a real goodbye to someone, you never see them again. Perhaps those are the words of the young and the unwise, but I will use them, nonetheless. My life, in all likelihood, will be short, but even if I live for a long time, we will never meet again. I say this because I want there to be a finality to this moment of shared tea and for you to feel an impressive sadness—who would I be if I weren't memorable?"

Cezal took his words without much of a reaction and felt like retorting that now it was Zamen who was wasting Cezal's time. He could deal with ego, arrogance even, yes, but to have someone then run you over in such a dismissive way? That was different, and Cezal no longer felt the need to entertain Zamen's fragility, though there was a part of him annoyed with himself for having expected the latter to be any different.

They made dry and stilted conversation for a few more minutes. Then Cezal went back to reading, and Zamen got some of the last of his things ready. Some minutes later, the train began to apply its breaks. Zamen got up and gathered his things. After a bit of time standing there, he slid open the door and faced the still-laying-down Cezal.

"I wish you all the best, my friend. Until next time, yes?" And then he winked and gave a little chuckle before starting out the door. A "wish me luck!" was his last parting phrase to Cezal while he slid the door closed.

Cezal didn't reply, though they both knew no reply was necessary. Soon after, the train came to a full stop, and after a short rest, they were picking up speed again. In the absence of the station lights, the dim glow of winter filled the room once more.

8

———

In the days following Zamen's departure, Cezal found himself spending more and more time with Alja. She, he found, was similar to Zamen in her cynicism and outlook, though she viewed herself very differently than did Zamen. She seemed to almost resent those who thought like ideologues; that is, those who think themselves to be a unique phenomenon. She also enjoyed trying to explain the people of Sectohal to him.

"We are alive during a strange time and are heading to a strange place," she said one day while they were having a lunch of bread, cheese, and cabbage. By then, the days were getting rather gloomier, and the sun rarely shown through the clouds. "You'll find that the people here feel empty in certain ways. This emptiness arises out of apathy, I think, but this apathy allows for a different, perhaps even deeper, authenticity that you'll not find in most people in other lands," she explained. "It is not really an authenticity with *others*, per se, but an authenticity with oneself—that's what that apathy affords us. People develop themselves differently when they grow up being completely, or near completely, honest with themselves. But perhaps most importantly of all, we don't waste our time trying to convince ourselves of untruths. We don't tell ourselves lies about who we are or who we should be. Looking at other people who lie to themselves out of some perceived moral obligation or out of worry of what others think strikes us as rather self-important."

Cezal paused a second and finished chewing his piece of bread. After he swallowed, he took a sip of tea. "Hm, that's an interesting idea. But why do you think there is this emptiness in the first place?"

Now Alja took some time to think and stared out the window for a moment. The scenery was beginning to look more dramatic, with the tops of low-rise mountains steeped in winter dreariness, the shadow of light snow lingering wherever on the mountainside the sun couldn't reach. "I'm not really sure. I think perhaps people have come to see their powerlessness."

"Powerlessness to what though?" he asked.

She shrugged. "Mm, it's a general powerlessness." She took a bite of bread and chewed well before continuing. "Not to the forces of nature, mind you, but rather to the forces that come from humans—the way we've come to structure our societies and institutions. I think we've forgotten the world only exists in our heads. All the things around us are only there because we perceive them." She quickly waved her hand. "But make no mistake—I'm not saying the world isn't real. I'm saying though that we've come to see the forces of society—*the system*, as people like to term it, as being outside of our control. And really, on an individual level, it is out of our control, but we also forget that all these systems are perpetuated by people too. There's nothing so special about them that ever makes them more-than-human. Perhaps then it's better said we've come to see the futility of grand efforts."

Cezal thought again for a second, and the train contin-ued its clacking. Of course, it always clacked, but in times of momentary silence, it became rather more noticeable. "Do you think that's overall a good or bad thing—viewing the world in such an unimpressed way?"

Alja gave a slight smile as though she had anticipated the question. "I don't know. I want to say it's overall not a good thing, though. Sometimes it feels almost like someone has scraped a fresco off a wall in order to reveal the bricks beneath it. Yes, now we see the bricks, but was it really worth it? There is joy to be found in regarding the fresco. So yes, there is a different kind of authenticity, but I don't know if it's really worth it in the end." She sighed. "Oh, but who am to say. I know *I* don't like it, which is a big reason why I left." She gave a sly, sardonic smile. "Maybe facing the vacuousness of existence is more other people's cup of tea," she said as she took a sip of her own.

* * *

The next morning, Cezal found himself talking with Alja over tea. That day had more of a glimmer to it. There had been snowfall the prior night, and so, combined with the clearer-than-usual sky, the sun had a particularness to it, standing out in the vast blue of day. Alja was someone who was comfortable with silence, much like, it would seem, most of the people Cezal had met on the train. She was staring out the window, deep in thought. He was casually reading the gazette from the town at the last stop—there never was much anything interesting in any of them.

Alja broke the silence. "You know, when I was younger, I was obsessed with Albert Camus, as any young person would be, I suppose. But what had really stuck with me was this part in one of his essays about actors. He had written that actors, the ones who truly live their role, *become* whom they act. They bring someone to life for two hours, and in that short while, live a lifetime. And that stuck with me. I wanted to live those thousand lives that an actor lives. It's why I had tried to make it as an actress for a while."

Cezal raised his eyebrows. "Oh really?"

She gave a light laugh. "Yes, but I must say, it was really rather ill-fated. I did a few plays and got a few minor roles, though none that paid. I realized there were better ways to try to live those different lives."

"Like how?" Cezal asked.

She shrugged. "Well, that's part of the reason I took up painting—they're like snapshots frozen in eternity, and yet, they also don't exist past themselves. What is depicted in a painting is all that there is. There's something strange, thinking about that while looking out the window at the world as it turns to winter. There's somewhat of an ephemeral quality to it—no day will look quite the same. At the same time, though, it will always repeat. It will always have that cycle." She shook her head. "I don't know. I often consider my temporal frame of reference. As people, we naturally experience the world one moment at a time, but have you ever tried to feel eternity?"

Cezal gave her a quizzical look.

"I don't mean it in some kind of trite, overly simplistic way. There is a real value in contemplating time, given we have only so much of it. Think about your frame of reference for everything and try to expand it to include all time—everything that has and will happen. Are you doing that?"

"Yes," replied Cezal, leaning back and crossing his legs.

"Okay, now, once you do that, you can look at the seasons and see winter in spring and spring in winter. You can see how they all exist in each other. Do you see what I mean?"

He shook his head. "Not quite."

She readjusted how she sat. "Okay. Imagine the present were all eternity. Yes?"

"Yes."

"Then that means all the things that have happened or ever will happen are considered to be at the same time."

"Mm, I suppose so."

She nodded. "So they all exist really at the same time, never changing. In that sense, then, one could say that the ephemeral and the eternal are really one in the same."

Cezal inhaled and raised his eyebrow. "I'll have to think about that more, but I suppose so. But what does that make our lives then?"

"What do you mean?" Alja asked.

"Well, if we don't consider our lives to be a cycle, if you were to take that perspective, what would that make our lives?"

"Well, that would make our lives infinitely short, I suppose. But then we have to ask if our lives aren't really cyclical. After all, what really is the difference between me and anyone else? If you accept that, at least theoretically, there's nothing about me that makes me different than you, past how I conceive of myself and the individual actions I take. Then, can it really be said I'm inherently different than you or anyone else from any other time? Really then, you would just be a different version of me, and I, a different version of you. Then, you could look at some human many thousands of years in the past and say that we are just a different version of them, no? If that were the case, then we would say that our lives are indeed cyclical, or rather not even that, but simply constantly existing."

Cezal took a sip of tea and nodded slowly. "Well, I'd have to think about that more. It's interesting you bring it up, though. I spoke about this same idea with another passenger some time ago," Cezal replied, leaning back and crossing his legs. "But, after the reflection I've done so far, I'm inclined to disagree. Can you really say that past our actions and self-conception, there's no difference between you and me? I have different memories, different values, different … many things than you. Certainly, there must be some accounting for that, wouldn't you say?"

She tilted her head slightly to the side. "Mm, I suppose, but still, is it not theoretically possible for you to have my same values, even if by chance? To that same end, there's no reason we couldn't have lived virtually the same life, however unlikely that may be."

Cezal smiled. "That's what my old companion said too, and for a while, I agreed, but that's the thing—we *didn't* live the same life, and I don't think we have all the same values."

Alja gave a reconciliatory shrug. "No, I understand that. My point is if it is theoretically possible, then there is nothing inherently preventing two people from being considered the same. I could go on with these questions of personal identity, but I think it wouldn't get anywhere productive. After a while, you just get into semantics, and the argument starts to lose its meaning."

Cezal nodded. "Hm, I suppose so. It *is* an interesting idea, though admittedly, I can't say I entirely follow your logic."

Alja smiled a bit. "Yes, well, I wouldn't break your head over it. I tend to go on tangential trains of thought. The point really was just to talk about the marvel of watching the seasons change."

Cezal smiled and looked out the window. "Yes, it is quite nice, isn't it."

They both looked out the window for some time, enjoying the light and the ephemerality of it all.

* * *

"Who?"

"*It is I, Patzal.*"

"Of course."

"*And I don't care of them. No one does.*"

"What do you mean 'care of them?'"

"*I mean exactly what I said. I don't care.*"

"*They should all die.*"

"*They pretend they care, but they don't. You don't care. I know that.*"

"But daddy, I do care."

"*No son, you don't care. You are miserable filth.*"

"No daddy."

"*YOU DON'T CARE.*"

"*Don't lie to me.*"

"But daddy I don't like how it feels."

"*You shouldn't.*"

"*I thought you were different, but no.*"

"*They die because you don't care. You are trash just like the others.*"

"*You die because you don't care.*"

"*Embrace it and die sooner.*"

"But daddy I love you."

"*Fuck you.*"

"*My son, you don't know love.*"

"*Don't cry.*"

" DON'T CRY."

"What a shameful being you are. I shouldn't have expected any more—"

"Mister… Mister!" Cezal broke in, upon entering his cabin and finding Patzal sitting on Zamen's former bed.

"What?" He shot Cezal a look of intense detestation. "Can't you see I'm busy?"

"There's no one there. It's just you and I, but you're scaring the other passengers. Can you be a bit quieter?"

Patzal continued to look intensely at Cezal, his mouth and nose starting to twitch in the process. Patzal looked into him, and Cezal immediately got up with his bag and tried to leave. Soon, a train police officer arrived—the same one who drank Cezal's wine.

"Is this the passenger giving you trouble?"

"Yes," Cezal replied.

"Come with me, if you would."

And Patzal went. And he looked at Cezal as he left, an intense smile plastered to his face. *Because he knows*, thought Cezal.

"Because he knows." Please, Cezal, what does that even mean? Don't be so dramatic.

Soon after, it was morning.

∗ ∗ ∗

The next day, over lunch, Cezal and Alja were talking again. Cezal mentioned Zamen once more, with his ideological plan and how, on the last night, he *revealed himself* to Cezal.

Alja gave somewhat of a knowing smile with tinges of disgust. "Mm, yeah, I suppose he's rather an unsavory figure, eh? Though he is right in that there were many warning signs. Deep down, surely you must have known he was pleasant with you while it was beneficial for him but if it became inconvenient, he would throw you away without a second's thought."

Cezal sighed, "I suppose I did, but I thought I could handle it—and I did, but of course, one doesn't enjoy feeling used."

She chuckled. "Yes, well, I suppose I understand. It's not enjoyable to discover the bad in others. The time before you really get to know someone is nice because you can fill them up with whomever you want them to be. Perhaps really, it can be used as a way of finding what you need in your own life. The kinds of people you're drawn to on a more surface-level way are probably then an indication of what you wish you had more of in yourself."

"How so?" Cezal asked.

"Well, you were drawn to Zamen for his free-spiritedness and confidence, were you not? That is why you were willing to put up with his arrogance."

"I suppose so."

Alja shrugged. "So perhaps that's an indication you should be more free-spirited and confident."

"Mm, perhaps that's true. I imagine my taking this trip in the first place is already rather a big step in that direction, though, wouldn't you say."

"Well, I would think so," Alja replied, "but of course, that's the kind of thing you need to answer for yourself."

"Yes, you're right. I didn't mean it in such a way," replied Cezal sitting in a relaxed manner. "What tendencies do you think you have?"

"I?" Alja asked, somewhat taken off guard.

"Well, yes," Cezal replied in as inoffensive a way as he could.

She nodded and looked out the window for a moment as she thought. "Well, I tend to enjoy my solitude. That is perhaps somewhat of a tendency in itself. I don't wish to sound melodramatic, so I will not go overly into it, but I know the kind of people I tend to draw are rather reserved."

"How do you mean?"

"Put simply, I suppose, we don't let each other into our lives too much."

"How do you feel about that?" Cezal inquired.

"Okay enough. If I were so dissatisfied by it, I would change how I am," Alja replied.

Cezal paused a moment. "I suppose then you feel rather in control of how you are?"

"Well, of course," replied Alja without hesitation, leaning forward. "It's a rather shameful thing to feel trapped by one's own personality, don't you think?"

Cezal paused and tilted his head to the side, "Mm, perhaps, though I think it is rather easier for some than others, wouldn't you say?"

"Yes, that is true." replied Alja waving her arm in a dismissive way. "Perhaps I shouldn't be so harsh. I'll amend my statement to being that it's rather shameful not to try to be in control of one's personality." She looked again out the window. "Do you feel trapped, Cezal?"

He threw up his head a bit and laughed, "Well certainly, you can see how that feels rather like a loaded question now, wouldn't you say?"

She chuckled. "Ah, well, forget what I've just said for the time being. It's not good to take anyone's opinion too seriously. *Do* you feel trapped?"

There was silence for a few moments as he thought. She watched the aspen trees go by in the early afternoon light, snow having dusted the ground and sticking in little clumps to the thin tree trunks that seemed so close to one another.

"Being trapped means there's something from which you can escape, does it not?" Cezal began. "But in the simplest sense of the question, what could I escape to?

Alja smiled. "Yes, that's rather true, I suppose. You can't escape yourself… That is something I learned the hard way. I am instead trying to learn to live with myself, to accept my emotions and my past. I avoided leaving Nesge until I was sure I wasn't leaving to try to escape. Because, as I'm sure you know, your problems will follow you wherever you go." She paused a moment and shifted to lean to the wall of the cabin with the window, resting her head on the window. "But to be honest, I get the sense that that's what you're trying to do by going to Briedavga… Or perhaps, it's not that you're avoiding something by leaving your hometown, but I think you expect to automatically find something there when really, other than its little idiosyncrasies and different landscape, after a while you'll find it not too drastically different from your own hometown." She made an expression as though to say, "But what can you do?"

"But regardless," she continued, "what do you expect to find there?"

Cezal leaned back and thought a second. "It's funny you bring it up—Zamen said the same thing."

"Ah," she laughed a bit, "well, I suppose even unpleasant people say something of value from time to time."

He smiled. "But yes," Cezal continued, "you've both raised good points. I really don't know. If anything, I suppose I'm trying to escape the monotony of my own life. I feel like there's more to be had, wouldn't you say?"

Alja paused and was still. "Perhaps so… But I think it will depend more on you than the place."

"Yes, you're right. I do know that. Of course, to apply that belief to one's life is a different matter, but nonetheless…" He trailed off. "Why are you going back to your childhood house?"

"To a certain extent, I suppose I'm traveling for the same reasons you are. But I think there's something to be said for 'coming full circle,' as they say, and for revisiting your past. When you can embrace it, that's when you know you can really move forward."

Cezal made a sign to show he agreed, and they both continued to look out the window at the winter unfolding before them. The train hadn't stopped now for over a day, and it would be at least one, if not two, more days before it would stop again.

* * *

The weather now was getting increasingly dreary and somber—at times even ominous, the landscape often shrouded in a withholding fog. On one such morning, while Cezal was reading a book and Alja was reading a newspaper from one of the bigger towns and both were in their pajamas enjoying their morning tea, Cezal asked her why she paints.

She looked at him for a moment and put down her paper.

"That's a good question." She paused for some time before taking a deep breath in. "I suppose in many ways I try to live through my art. Perhaps in that sense, my paintings can be considered something of a corollary to my own life." She paused a bit more and looked out the window, half thinking of what to say next and half wondering if she would continue at all. "You know after you stare long enough at a painting, and I mean *really* just sit still and stare at it for a long time, its color and form start to fade together and become nearly indistinguishable. Eventually, the frame starts to move into

the wall behind it, and so too does the canvas until it envel-
ops your whole field of vision and a new, blank canvas that is
both there and not there faces you. If you keep staring long
enough, you forget it was an optical illusion to begin with,
and you get used to this new, unstimulating plain. If you do
this enough, you eventually start to feel that the blankness
is more real than the vivid painting. That lack stares at you
with each passing day. I stared at it for quite a while. I do
not know how long exactly, but after I got comfortable with
it, I ached to fill it with something. So, I dreamt of beauty
and flowers and fields, sunshine that warms your face, and a
family of my own to fill the painting. I dreamt of belonging
and neededness. Such a place doesn't exist. And nor would
I exist in that place since it's so idealized, but I dream it
nonetheless. And it is beautiful… It is beautiful because it
can't be real. Because it can't exist, nothing can tarnish it."

She smiled softly and looked at Cezal.

"Yes. It can never be real, but it is more beautiful than
anything else—more beautiful than anything I could ever
paint. And because of that, it is more real than even my
own life. I truly enjoy it. Over time, I've come to live tucked
away, between the shades of meaning, in the various angles
of shadows cast onto the frontiers of reality. I swim in the
never-ending ocean of half-existence. I used to believe there
is a shore, and if I swam long enough and hard enough, I'd
find the beach. But I no longer believe in shores or beaches."
She took a deep breath and closed her eyes before continuing.
"To swim in nothingness. To breathe the water in and feel it
with your entire being. That is when you begin to dream. And
after you begin to dream, you begin to live in the quiet folds
of reality, tucked away and hidden from everyday life." She
tilted her head slightly and smiled. "We never truly possess

that which can be taken from us, and no one can ever take our dreams away. That's why I dream of beauty and of people and meadows and sun and meaning. It's how I paint my life with tints from beyond the color spectrum." She paused a second and looked at Cezal's rather puzzled face. "To answer your question more directly, I suppose by painting, I'm able to continue to explore a reality that is greater than myself. It's a very gratifying experience."

9

——

Cezal and Alja walked idly back to their respective cabins from the dining car. The lights on the walls of the train were warm and inviting. Light danced across the lacquered, wood paneling that lined the car, and the warm interior contrasted pleasantly with the snowstorm outside. In the dining car, every once in a while, when there was a lull in the conversation, one could hear the hollow sound of wind and the clack of the train among the clinking of cutlery.

They walked past some cabins, mostly empty, filled only with nicely made beds or clean, maroon benches, as this stretch of the train ride wasn't too busy, and most of the occupants aboard were still enjoying dessert or an after-dinner coffee. One cabin, however, caught Cezal's eye—not due to anything particular or necessarily even visibly eye-catching about it, but rather because of the stark bleakness emanating from it. Bekochan was there, curled up in a ragged ball at the end of one of the benches, his face smeared against the window.

They stopped. "Oh, Alja, look at him. I think he needs some company."

She looked dolefully through the window at his wasting figure. "Perhaps you should. You know him better. I'll take our stuff to my cabin and stay there. You come when he's ready."

Cezal slid open the door and sat down, opposite Bekochan, who was by the window at the end of the cramped cabin.

"Good evening, Bekochan. How are you doing tonight? Did you get some dinner?"

Bekochan continued to stare dimly out the window.

"Bekochan! Are you okay?" he asked, leaning over to shake his shoulder, trying to roll it to get his head to face him. Bekochan tried to open his eyes more and propped his head up with one of his hands, keeping it semi-upright by grabbing a fistful of hair on the side of his head tight. This seemed to make him more alert.

"Bekochan, you've drunk too much again. Try to stay awake. Have you had anything to eat tonight?"

"Mm, yeah I had some crackers… I have more. Do you want some?"

"No. No, I'm quite fine, Bekochan. But thank you. Perhaps you should eat them."

"Heehh, yeah, you want that, don't you. Ha-ha, yea. No, I—no, I'm kind of hungry."

He sloppily unwrapped the remaining crackers and began to eat them, making a mess of crumbs over his drab knit sweater and the equally drab floor.

"Are you okay, Bekochan?" Cezal asked emphatically.

Suddenly, his face darkened more, and he quickly forgot his excitement over the crackers. He gritted his teeth and twisted his head. "I, my girlfriend, she doesn't want me any-more. And… I'm…" His *mmm* transitioned into a sob as he crumpled into himself.

What a sad sap. Cezal was appreciative this wasn't his life. He had someone to spend his time with, and he wasn't a drunken mess. What girlfriend could he be talking about? Bekochan, the dirty weirdo who was always running his hand back through his hair and rubbing his oily face—the one who smelled as though he hadn't taken a shower for weeks. He had his charm during his lucid times, but how often was that?

How hard Bekochan's life is. How empty. How sad. And why should one have to suffer despair? Cezal asked himself. *Do I see a meaningful future for this man? No. Does he? No. So for what then does he live?*

But Cezal, wait a second, he thought. *Who are you to be thinking of these things for him? It is he who must decide for himself.*

Sure, but why is that? What chance is there for him to have a happy ending? He has told me before he wants to die.

Yes, but that is when he was spiraling. There are his better days.

But do the better days make up for it? Is it really worth it? A utilitarian would have had him killed long ago.

Yes, but utilitarians aren't exactly the bastions of morality, now are they?

Well, that's true, but still. If I can be sure that, if he were of sound mind when he's in these spirals and could look at himself and his life, he would want to die, then I can make that decision for him.

Well, you can always make that decision for him or anyone for that matter. But you will have to live with the weight of your action.

Bekochan belched and rolled to face the window again.

But how is it wrong to put someone out of their misery? I would want the same if it were I in his position.

Yes, but you know that's easy to say when you aren't *in his position.*

Yes, that's true. But do I really see him getting better? What will I, or anyone else, ever do for him? I don't even know where he's going or why he's on the train.

Cezal broke the silence. "Bekochan, why are you on the train? Are you going to see family or anyone?"

There was no answer, but only a shudder and harder sob after mentioning family. He was clutching a pearl necklace in his hands. Cezal had never seen it before, but it seemed not the time to bring it up.

So he's got no one.

You know in your heart, Cezal, the conclusion you're coming to. You know I won't support it. But you also know there are times when you must go against your conscience—against your gut feeling.

Cezal's chest tightened, and a wave of anxiety washed over him. The past was gone and the future ended with Bekochan.

This is the point. This is the point where one must overcome oneself and do what needs be done, even if it's evil. But, how could I live with myself if I thought I were evil? No, one must be selfless. One must be greater.

Cezal shook his head forcefully.

Forget me—I don't exist. I must do.

"Say Bekochan, do you have anything I could drink?"

"Yeah," rolled out of his mouth, and he seemed to perk up at the prospect of Cezal's drinking something. He managed to rotate his torso to fumble around in his bag. After some moments of watching him try to search through his dirty belongings, he brought out a surprisingly nice-looking, half-empty jar of what he said was horseradish spirits.

"Did you make this yourself?" He seemed to be getting more of a grip and was able to respond.

"No, it was a gift," he slurred.

"All right. Well I think you've probably had enough for now, but I'll have some if you don't mind."

Hah, Cezal, please. Are you really trying to get yourself drunk beforehand? Just because you are *a feeble idiot doesn't mean you have to* act *like one.*

Cezal's hands shook as he poured the spirits into a glass teacup.

No, I know what must be done. It's you *who needs to be quiet.*

Ah, your conscience, yes. What would you do without me? Okay, Cezal, have it your way. I'll shut up. Gladly. Just know this is one of those moments you'll always regret.

He had five shots or so in the span of ten minutes and tried to make stilted conversation with Bekochan, but the slob couldn't muster much other than sobs and slurred half-thoughts. It served to distract Cezal, though.

Perhaps, he thought, *it would be better if Bekochan had more in his system? Then he wouldn't realize what's happening as much.*

"Hey, Bekochan, why don't you have some shots with me? You've eaten those crackers, so I imagine you can handle some more, eh?" Cezal flashed him a smile that masked the fear on the lips but did little for the rest of Cezal's anxiety-splattered face.

Bekochan gave an ill-formed smile back but still made no eye contact. Cezal wondered when the alcohol would start to kick in and took three more consecutive shots with Bekochan.

Give it a couple of more minutes, then get the train police. They'll take care of the actual act.

Ah, passing the buck are we, Cezal? Yes, get them to do the dirty work. Maybe then, when you consider how it feels

*to kill someone, you can assure yourself it wasn't you who
technically killed him.*

I told you to be quiet.

His eyes looked sharply at Bekochan's. "So I guess this is it."

Did I say that out loud?

Yes, Cezal, you did. But it doesn't matter.

*Maybe this is what people mean when they say someone
was too good for the world. Oh, poor Bekochan. But it's too
late… Yes, it was always too late.*

"Bekochan… Bekochan! I'm going to get some hot water
at the end of the car. Do you want some?"

"No."

Cezal stepped out of the stale air of the cabin and paid
attention to his gait, concentrating on his feet as he walked
down the hall. A few cabins down, he found an older couple
enjoying their evening tea and reading. He knocked and slid
the door open enough that his face could fit in a bit to talk
to the couple.

"Good evening, madame and sir. I apologize for dis-
turbing you. I'm with a passenger a few cabins up and he's
gotten rather drunk and seems unstable. I worry he could
cause some trouble. I need to stay with him to keep an eye.
Would one of you kind souls mind informing one of the train
policemen? It's cabin number twenty-seven. Yes, he's the one
wearing a rather worn, red knit sweater."

The older man, sitting upright in his seat, adjusted his
bifocals and began to speak. "I—I'll let them know. You get
back to your cabin. Number twenty-seven, you say?"

"That's the one. Thank you for your help, sir, and again,
sorry to you both for the disruption."

Cezal walked back, touching the walls as he did in order
to stabilize himself. Eventually, he came to the cabin and slid

open the door to find a passed out Bekochan. "Bekochan!" he said. "Stay awake! Trust me. It's better that you stay awake. Bekochan!"

"Mmhrm."

Cezal poured himself into his previous seat.

"Bekochan, come on. I think I saw a train policeman walking around. You need to get yourself together." That seemed to get his attention a bit, but there was, of course, only so much one could do at this point. Cezal continued coaxing him for the next couple of minutes and was soon interrupted by a knock at the sliding door. The train policeman stood tall and, unlike the other policeman Cezal talked with, this one wasn't borderline-gangly but instead filled up the doorframe.

What have I done?

The policeman took a deep, quick breath through the nose and looked at Cezal, then to Bekochan.

"Is this him?" the officer asked, gesturing with his chin.

"Yes," replied Cezal.

"Sir, please come with me," the officer said as he reached for Bekochan's arm.

"Hrmm," was all Bekochan managed to get out, followed by his arm, half raised at the officer's general direction.

"I need you to get up and come with me," he said.

Cezal, in turn, got up, seeing where this was going, and did his best to contain the urge to flee. "I should get back to my own cabin, officer. Do you have the situation under control?"

The officer looked at Cezal, standing from the doorway. His upper cheek twitched. Annoyance tinged his voice. "If you must. I have backup coming soon. Do you know where his ticket is?" He pointed his head at Bekochan.

"I'm afraid not," Cezal slurred, attempting to keep his balance. "I just met him."

His eyes narrowed. "Very well."

"May I get back to my cabin, officer?"

He continued to block the exit. "What is your name? Where are your ticket and papers? Empty your pockets."

"My name is Cezal Iktoleu, sir."

Once the officer grunted in acknowledgment, Cezal proceeded to do as he was told and was vaguely glad he left his valuables with Alja before coming. There was a pocketknife, a clean handkerchief, a few coins, and, most importantly, his ID, stamped travel papers, and a validated ticket. Cezal put it all on the table and gave the policeman his ID and papers, taking care to present it to him with both hands. He looked over them intently, glancing over every once in a while to make sure Bekochan was still sleeping and Cezal hadn't moved.

The wind seemed stronger then than it had before and filled Cezal's dull ears. The policeman brusquely gave him back the papers, and Cezal quickly put them all into his pocket again. The policeman seemed hesitant but let him go. Cezal stumbled out, and relief washed over him. The train seemed shakier than before, and the lights brighter, too. He felt people staring at him. The man with the bifocals surely shook his head reproachfully as he passed. A couple of minutes later, he was back in the cabin, and Alja was already asleep.

* * *

The next morning, Cezal woke up late, and the light in the room pierced him as sharp sound would one's ears. Sometime later, Alja came with tea, and she got to telling him a story from when she was a child, seemingly unaware of his state.

"When I was younger," she began, sitting down with her hands around the cup of tea, looking out the window, "there was once a drought that lasted nearly three years. It made most of the grasses and crops die. Most of the pine trees were able to survive, but by the end of second year, they only had brown needles left. It was a time of dust and despair for all in the community. That whole area had been cleared and was filled with fields as far as the eye could see. I was rather young then—probably no older than ten. We lived with my grandparents at the time, and my grandpa, for whom the farm was his pride and joy, would often sit out on the porch on his rocking chair, looking at the dying forest and the cracked, dirt fields. I remember he would sit in the summers, during the afternoons, and the heat would swell up from the ground, and in the flat, barren distance, you could see, among the dry shrubbery that dotted the landscape, the heat lines rise up.

"The heat of such days was unbearable, and we all walked around with wet cloths on our necks and thin linens my mom had received some years before as a gift. The town was small and poor—a ranching town of what was increasingly seeming like a bygone era. During the drought, no one went outside unnecessarily, especially during July and August, when the sun was so intense. But in the evenings, when the sun would paint the sky with vivid colors and a hot breeze would brush itself over the land, somewhere far in the distance, the dogs would start to bark. They howled at the moon as it came into view. I would often join my grandpa out there, pulling up a chair next to him. He was a man of few words, and so the time was punctuated mostly by the crackle of the hot fields. One time though, when the dogs had started their evening barking, he shifted how he was sitting a bit and turned to face me. 'Do you know what the dogs are calling for, Alja?' he asked. I told him I didn't know. He turned his head back to face the fields and the sound of the distant dogs. 'They call for you, my dear,' he said, rocking gently in his rocking chair. No one I knew had ever seen the dogs or known why they were there. Only the crickets and the howl of the oncoming night was to be heard through the valley. He smiled softly and repeated, half to me and half to himself, 'They call for you.'"

Alja wistfully smiled as she finished recounting the experience, leaning back against the wall of the car as she continued looking out the window at the passing winter that unfolded before them. Cezal seemed neither to be fully awake nor really in the mood, so she stopped talking there and simply basked in the memory a bit longer.

* * *

Later that day, when the afternoon sun was low enough that it showered its light at a rather stark angle, making the trees cast shadows on each other, Alja began to talk with Cezal again. Still, he seemed somewhat preoccupied, to speak in understatement. They both sat at the table with tea.

Cezal stared into his cup. "I've been thinking a lot about what we and Zamen talked about—that there's no substance to us as people. That we're only what we do and what we project, and that there's no real person underneath."

Alja stared at him. "And do you agree?"

Cezal pushed his mouth slightly to the side. "Yes, I think so. There's who we think we are and our natural inclinations, but our actions are just projections of that person we think we are. There's nothing baser about it. I suppose in that way, we are really just self-perpetuating ideas, wouldn't you say?"

Alja took a sip of tea and tilted her head a bit to the side. "I do agree," she began. "It's an idea I was very fond of when I was younger—the concept that we're just ideas. It does make you think, doesn't it?" She smiled a bit and looked out the window at the passing trees, spattered with ambered light and shadows. "It raises some important questions, though, and makes you reconsider reality and how much of it is in your head. I enjoyed, like I've talked about before, thinking of my dreams about the world and making them more real than reality. There was a person I wanted myself to be, and I tried my best to forget who I *was* then. Sometimes I felt like I was successful in this undertaking. I felt like the person I imagined myself to be was more real than the person I more effortlessly was." She paused and looked at Cezal.

He seemed to be engaging with what she said.

She sighed somewhat wistfully and continued. "Yes, but it was rather ill-fated. The person I wanted to be wasn't a separate person from who I already was. It was simply a version of me who didn't have the same faults I saw myself as having. Do you see how that's rather dooming from the start?"

"Not quite," Cezal replied.

"It meant I wasn't really making a new person. It means I was trying to get rid of myself by latching onto someone new who was created through the template of the old me. It means that my new me I wanted to be was built on the foundation of my same old faults."

"And what were you trying to do with your new you? Whom were you trying to become?" Cezal asked.

Alja shook her shoulders. "Oh, what does anyone want to be? I was no different. I didn't like that I was shy and self-conscious or that I overthought things. I was rather the self-destructive type. I always felt like people would leave me once they found someone better, so even with my closest friends, there was a part of me that was always waiting for the day they would pretend they never knew me."

Cezal nodded his head. "So what happened then?"

"Well, I tried to be more confident. I made it a point not to overthink. I told myself not to care about what others thought, and there would be those that don't like me, and I need to accept that and move on."

Cezal nodded. "Sounds like good advice."

Alja shook her shoulders again, "It was, yes. But I found it rather tiring to try and be this whole new person and have this entirely new conception of the world and the relation-ships around me. In the end, I did improve for the better, but it's more that I was less shy and cared less about the opinions of others, and not that I simply shed my former personality." She paused a bit and admired the scenery and the twinkle of the sun again. "I think there's a basic mood that pervades each person. Everyone has their own feel to them. Perhaps those who truly know themselves have been able to figure out why they have this mood or why they have their inclinations, but for the majority of us, myself included, you get to the point where you find this mood, and then you can't go much further. It's still leftover. I suppose you can't really change what you're not conscious of and what you don't understand, so that's why it's pretty hard to *really* change who you are."

Cezal nodded and sat in silence for some time, the train simply passing through the ever-isolated terrain.

"Do you think there ever could be anything essential to a person?"

"Well, how do you mean?" she replied.

"I mean—" Cezal began, before stopping himself. "I suppose I don't really mean that. Do you think it's possible to stop being a human?"

She tilted her head and smiled. "To exist outside of that?"

"Yes," he replied.

Alja threw her head up in subdued laughter. "Ah, well, I mean really this is one of those subjects where any meaning is likely to be lost in semantics, so I hesitate to say either yes or no because I don't know what, to you, it means to be human." She squinted her eyes and leaned in a bit as she said this last part. "What I can say is that, especially when I was younger, I did try to challenge what it meant to be a person. For a few years, that was my mission in life."

"And how's that?" Cezal asked.

"Well," replied Alja, "I suppose it was the natural next point to go to. After I felt like I couldn't change who I was, I tried to break out of the framework of what it means to be a human. It started with asking myself things like 'where do I end and others begin?' and 'to what extent am I a reflection of my environment and to what extent is the environment a reflection of myself?' I experimented with such thinking.

"And as time went on, it increasingly felt as though my life were some kind of experimental art exhibition. Of course, I became inclined to see myself as though a spectator to this exhibition, though then it wouldn't be that *I* was solely the art exhibition, but also a spectator. So I did my best to try and not be the human observer." She paused to take a sip of tea, and Cezal did the same. "As you can probably surmise, it was often a frustrating and rather unwieldy process. There were times, though, when I felt like I understood reality and myself in quite a unique way. I would suggest anyone do it—you begin to learn more about yourself through it. It's a strange feeling to begin to look at your life in such a detached way and to purposefully try to conceive of yourself not as a human, but rather as a two dimensional being no more than a complex idea." She trailed off for a moment. "It gives you a strange feeling of power over your own life too. And you start to view your life in its finitude. You realize you have a definite start and end to your existence, and there are no do-overs or making up for lost time; you truly can waste your life away, or you can make it into something amazing. In both cases, one is left wondering, 'So what?'"

Cezal nodded and looked at her for a few moments more. "That's an interesting way of viewing things," he finally replied. "I assume you put a lot of this process into your art?"

Alja smiled in response. "Well, of course. It changed the purpose of my art. I tried to *find myself* through it, as clichéd as that sounds. Really though, I think that's what many artists do. I don't use my art to represent myself or my experience either, though. I have no desire to immortalize my perspective of the world. No." She shook her head. "It's more that I used my art to *be* that extra-reality. It's not meant to represent anything. Even though I often paint what may look like landscapes, I'm not trying to represent whatever landscape is in my mind. It likely looks like a landscape, yes, but it is not a landscape that I paint. There is only the painting itself and its own reality. The painting is both a means and an end in itself. Because there *is* a reality that isn't so concrete that exists—you just have to figure out the right way to go about perceiving it. It's my way of creating meaning in my life. And besides, I would be lying if I said I find much meaning in anyone's life, so art is certainly an important way of 'making' meaningfulness for me, so to speak."

Cezal nodded, though he had nothing to add.

* * *

The darkness filled the train cabin, and Cezal lay in bed in a tight ball, trying to stay warm. He didn't know what caused the sudden change in temperature, but his sheets were no longer enough to keep him warm at night.

I hope you're happy with what you've done.

I'm not.

Yes, well, I hope you think it was worth it.

Cold emptiness filled the room.

Well… was it?

I don't know.

Oh, don't be so shameful, little flower. Stand tall and proud. I hope you are proud of what you've done. And besides, he's not alive anymore, so how can he be real?

But he was real then.

Oh fuck off, Cezal. Work with me. You're insufferable enough as it is. He's gone. And you're the reason for that. You've lived a rather insignificant life. You should view this perhaps as your crowning accomplishment. I should make you a little medal for it. You can hang it up in your little attic in Briedavga. Then when some nice little visitor comes by, you can proudly show it off. Eh? Would that make you feel special and all warm inside?

Cezal steeped in the tar of regret.

My, my, what a sad little flower you are. You'll have to forgive me, dearest one, if I ask you to put your big boy boots on. If you're going to sick the train police on Bekochan, you need to accept the consequences.

A cold breeze blew through the cabin.

What? You didn't realize that the logic you use to dehu-manize others applies to yourself as well? Oh, but my dear, you had that coming. My, my, what a regrettable little existence you are, eh?

The night seeped ever further into Cezal.

Well, you know what, I'll give you an out. You deserve it, don't you think? Yes. Pretend it never happened. Wipe it from your memory. Don't tell Alja—no, you can't do that. Never acknowledge it ever. If she asks where he is, you have to pretend you don't know. Just say you talked with him a bit, and he fell asleep, and that's when you came back. Right? Because that is what happened, after all.

But don't you think it's strange she hasn't asked about him at all yet? It's been a few days now.

You think she knows?

I don't know.

Hah! I hope she does. What do you think she'd do?

I don't know.

No. I think you have some concrete ideas.

The clack continued.

But that's okay. You don't have to tell me what you think. I'll just tell you what I think. I think she'd kill you, no? I mean, evidently, it's rather easy. She seems like someone who's rather confident with her views of the world. It almost seems like she doesn't think other people are real, don't you think? What makes you think you're real, dearest Cezal? Eh?

What makes you think you're real?

Oh please, Cezal, spare me. No need to try and impress me with some half-baked, snide remark. No. I'd tell you what you are, but I don't think I need to. You go to sleep now, yes? Feel the cold in your bones. Maybe that will toughen your indomitable spirit.

It was now winter, and a thin layer of snow that didn't melt in the daytime covered the ground. It was rather dry snow, though, and tended to crust over from the partial melt in the day. This, in turn, made it such that, on particularly blustery occasions, the wind would pick up millions upon millions of little snow crystals and throw them about, blowing them like waves through the air, churning and flowing through the vast, wintery expanses, sounding like wind through pine needles.

Both Cezal and Alja enjoyed the early afternoon on the train when the sun was low on the horizon, but not low enough for the light to turn the gleaming yellowish red of the before twilight. In either case, though, as usual, it was rather overcast.

"I haven't told you the story about the fisherman and the whale before, have I?" Alja asked, seated at the table.

Cezal opened his eyes from his half-sleep.

"No, I don't think you have."

"Ah, well then, let me liven the cabin up with something of a tale," Alja began, smiling. "It's a purportedly true story that comes from the West, from somewhere in the mountains between two great seas. My mother used to tell it to me. It's rather well-known, I think.

"There was once a poor fisherman who lived in a small town and eked out a living fishing for cod on his little boat. Day in and day out, he would venture to sea. Such was his life for as long as he could remember. One spring day, when he was older and less filled with the energy of youth, he met a whale who was wonderful in every imaginable way. As time went on, they grew increasingly close with one another. The whale enjoyed spending its time with someone who appreciated the sea so much, and the man enjoyed being with someone who made him feel young again. Eventually, they fell in love, and the whale tried to convince the man to live with it in the sea. Of course, that would be impossible. He couldn't breathe underwater."

Cezal gave a questioning look. "So the whale can talk, but he can't breathe underwater?"

"Oh, I know," she laughed, "but it's a children's story. You have to suspend your disbelief."

He nodded.

"Well," Alja continued, "the seasons came and went, and the fisherman and whale met every day, sharing their afternoons with each other. Their longing to be together grew stronger and stronger, and eventually, the fisherman decided he would go to a witch to see if he could get some potion to be able to breathe underwater.

"He went to see the witch and was told that there was only one such potion for his scenario but it would last only for one day and could only be effective when the full moon fell on the summer solstice. Of course, through the serendipity found only in children's stories, the next week just so happened to have a full moon that fell on the summer solstice. The fisherman agreed readily, but the witch stopped him, seeing his eagerness. She told him that if he wished to get the potion, he would have to give up everything he had, but for the clothes he was wearing that very day.

"The fisherman, in his blinding love, decided to go through with the deal, and so the witch gave him the potion: a thick blue liquid in a glass vial.

"He couldn't wait for the day he would finally be with the whale, and the whale too waited eagerly for his arrival. Finally, the solstice came, and the fisherman drank the potion. It worked perfectly, of course, and he dove into the pristine ocean and swam to the whale. He explained that he had only one day, and this would be the only time the potion could work. The whale, of course, was distraught, but they decided they would have to make the most of it." Alja nodded. "And they did. They saw the coral reefs and algae and sea urchins. They saw the wondrous fish and other sea life and lived that day as they had lived no day before—so happy to finally be together. It was a marvelous twenty-four hours by any standard. Of course, though, as with any day, it was to end. And so, as time began to run out, the fisherman swam for the beach. He and the whale embraced one last time before he climbed back ashore, crying as he did. Once he got out of the water, he sat on the beach and continued to cry throughout the night." Alja shrugged, smiling. "And thus ends the story."

Cezal knit his eyebrows. "That's a rather abrupt ending. What happened to the fisherman and the whale afterward?"

She tilted her head to the side. "There was no afterward."

"What do you mean there was no afterward?" Cezal replied. "It isn't as though he dropped dead after getting back ashore."

"Well, no, but it's a story, Cezal. The fisherman and whale only exist in the story."

"But you said this was a true story—some sort of thin-ly-veiled fiction."

"Well, some version of it happened, but through the years, obviously quite a few details have changed. I mean, for heaven's sake, Cezal, one of the protagonists is a whale."

"Yes, but the point is, these were real people," Cezal pressed.

"Yes, I suppose they were real," she replied, somewhat annoyed.

"And so their lives must have continued past the story then."

She scoffed lightly. "Well, yes, from the practical point of view perhaps, but that's the beauty of the story. Because of the story, they exist together for only one day, one wonderful day filled with love and the wonders of the ocean. What more could you ask for?"

"I don't really agree with you. I mean, how can one simply say they didn't exist further?"

Alja sighed and shook her head and stared out the window a bit. "You've said it yourself, Cezal; people are ideas. And an idea can start or end at any point in time at a moment's notice. Perhaps I'm so forceful about this point because I have chosen to view myself in this way. I've decided I am an idea, and thus, my life, being that it is the expression of ideas, is itself art. When I can muster it up in myself, I live in the most beautifully human way possible—at least that's what I try to do. In doing so, I try to make my life a magnum opus, so to speak. The story I just told encapsulates this because the characters don't exist past themselves."

Cezal nodded. Alja paused and sighed, shifting how she sat on the bed.

"I try to love all living things with my entire being because otherwise, how would I stop myself from forsaking them and wishing it all to disappear? Some laugh so as not to cry. I love so as not to hate." She paused. "I make myself love when I see myself start to curse the world and all those in it."

The train clacked.

"Why do you start to curse the world?"

She shrugged.

"Because people are disappointing. There comes a time when you see around you the emptiness of most people's words. They used to have weight, and when you were a kid—you listened to them with your being. But after long enough, you found yourself abandoned in them. Especially their promises. Words are indeed cheap, and so I no longer give them much thought. Through the virtue of my constantly having challenged what it means to be human when I was younger, I've been able to cultivate in myself a vast interior world, with an ocean deep and blue, with calm waters and stormy waves; with the scorching sun at the surface and darkly salted, cold depths, far from the sounds of the world. I fill it at times with glaciers and at others with sunrises. I, too, have made a forest, deep and filled with life. It is full of sounds that permeate the night, morning dew, and deep, foggy darkness.

"And I've explored the forest and the ocean a thousand times, and a thousand times they've explored me too. *There* lies the depth of my being—the depth of my story. It is beyond the emptiness of words. I've found depth in that which is shallow, and I've made it my home. Perhaps that sounds rather self-important, but I don't mean it as such. It is how I've come to make sense of my life. I've found my interior world more fulfilling than the external one. And so it's in the same way that I can look at a short story, like that of the fisherman and the whale, and consider it complete."

Cezal nodded. "I see. But do you think this makes it more difficult for you to find meaning in the world, seeing that you keep it at arm's length?"

Alja sighed slowly and deeply, looking out the window at the passing trees dusted in pristine snow. "Yes, I suppose so. But one learns to keep others distant after a while. They have disappointed me, and I have disappointed them. You know, it reminds me of a story."

Cezal smiled. "You sure seem to like stories."

"Well, yes," Alja replied, looking at him like he shouldn't be surprised. "They're nice. They have internal cohesion and provide nice allegories to whatever point I'm trying to make. But anyhow, I suppose this is more of a personal anecdote than a story." She shook her head. "Regardless, I once went to an inn on the side of a road while traveling when I was younger—when I was moving to Nesge. It was in a pine forest, and this inn functioned like a rest stop with a tavern and a small store attached to it. As an attraction, there was a grizzly bear in a metal cage near the entrance. It was emaciated and mangy. It barely moved, with a ring through its nose for when they paraded it around and with matted fur that was gone in many parts, revealing pinkish skin and patches of sores covered in flies. It didn't respond to calls or jeers or any noise. The only food it got was the scraps the restaurant patrons gave, and even then, it barely lifted its head to eat.

"I was leaving the restaurant as the owner was outside throwing it food. Some of it landed on its back, but the bear didn't shake it off. Flies quickly swarmed it, but many more stayed on his sores. The bear took a few bites of what landed near his mouth. There was such sadness in his eyes. He wanted to die, you could tell. I asked the owner how he could keep a bear like this, and he replied coolly, 'Yes, I know it's not great. Ah, but such is the life of a beast.' I was rather taken aback by such a flippant response, but he was already walking back inside, and I didn't pursue it further. I left that same day. Of course, I had wanted to do something, but what good could I do? I didn't kid myself that I would save that bear by giving it some fleeting connection with a caring person. I probably could have pet it. That would have been stupid to do, I know. It probably would have bitten my arm off in defense. At least then I'd have known it was truly alive, I suppose." She looked down into her cup for a moment.

She looked back up at Cezal, who nodded in an attempt to show his engagement with the story.

"No," she continued. "The bear was not my responsibility. I left it and have faced no repercussions for having done so. Nor, of course, did the restaurant owner. It's surely dead by now—this was at least fifteen years ago. But it's not about responsibility or lack thereof. It is about something wrong happening and allowing it to continue. It doesn't matter if I would have stopped it or someone else, or even the bear himself. But it was a problem that needed a solution. And it was a problem that no one fixed. I should have gotten a gun and shot it in the night. I could have gotten away rather easily. None of the other patrons would have suspected me. I just would have had to run back to my room quickly. Ah, the owner would have accused me, though, I'm sure, because of my comment from earlier in the day. But he would have no proof, and he wouldn't have been able to rally the rest of the lodgers because deep down, they thought the bear was better off dead too. And even those who would have viewed my killing of the bear as the destruction of property, they wouldn't have cared that much. It wasn't their bear. But I'm getting off-topic. The point is, in the face of injustice, I did nothing. There's no justification for that. I'm not beating myself up about it. It would be rather self-important to put all the moral weight of doing *the right thing* on oneself solely. But there's still a hollow failure I have for not having acted." She looked down and pursed her lips to the left. "And a failure in humanity too. Everyone else there is just as much at fault as I am."

She sighed again, and silence descended for a few moments as Cezal noticed a muffled conversation happening next door.

"Yes, perhaps there is that failure," Cezal broke in. "But there too is a weight that comes with doing the right thing, if by right, you mean killing the bear. Of course, I suppose you could have freed it, though that would have been a far messier situation. I suppose then, in times like that, it's not as much about making a courageous, even selfless, decision as much as it's about making an existential decision for another being. I'm not saying it can't, or even shouldn't, be done—making such decisions, that is, but there is a weight that comes with it. It's a heavy one."

Alja nodded, and they both sat for a few moments, the train clacking and the afternoon light getting increasingly golden in its overcast way.

"Well," Alja began, looking up at Cezal, "in that case, it sounds like there's no good decision. If we accept that, then I suppose the next question is, how can anyone be good?"

"I suppose no one can be good in that case," replied Cezal. "But how is that a fair assessment, really? How can we say that all people are bad?"

"Well," began Alja somewhat dismissively, "I don't think it's that people are bad or good. We simply are. As we live life, we have to make decisions, and many of them have no good options, and so there's a certain weight to existence that naturally comes with it. Certainly then, it doesn't make one bad to make the best choices they can. You play the cards you're dealt. There's perhaps some somber comfort in that."

They sat again in silence, watching the trees and snow as afternoon turned into evening. Cezal laid down in bed, and Alja stayed seated, cupping her glass cup with her hand as she stared out the window.

"Sometimes," she said, "I wish I could go back to when I was younger, when the future was full of hope and possibility.

I love it. I really love it so much. I often try to convince myself that I am back—that I'm in my youth and my family and friends are around me, and we're all looking forward to the future. Often, when I'm exploring my interior world, I do it as a small child exploring it the first time." She sighed again. "It's important to remind oneself how that felt. That's also why I like the period of time right before you go to sleep— that twilight hour when anything can be, and you can live in the comfort of your memories… I have some version of that when I live in my internal world, and it's nice, but it's a different kind of reality than that of romanticized memories."

"Hope," began Cezal, "as trite as it sounds, is, I suppose, what keeps one youthful. It's rather easy to give it up and detach—to think of all that's passed and all that you will never get back, all that could have been. It's comforting in a way, but it wears you down over time."

Alja sighed. "What a tiring subject it all is. All the sadness, all the melancholy." She continued to stare out the window. "Perhaps, Cezal, one day I'll leave."

He turned his head from his supine position to face her. "Where will you go?"

She shrugged. "It doesn't really matter. But I won't be here, in this world. Perhaps I should stop trying. I used to think it ignoble to try to flee from oneself—like an act of defeat." She sighed again and looked down. "But I'm tired now, Cezal, and I see now that there is no such thing as honor or dereliction. There is only emptiness."

Enough time passed that her tea was completely cold when she spoke again. "Are you still awake, Cezal?"

"Yes."

"You know, I've gotten used to the idea of growing old and dying alone. At times it gets to me, but I've mostly come to accept it, and it doesn't bother me much anymore. Another person will not complete me. I know that well. Though what I fear is that I am not complete on my own, and that is a rather cutting idea. I suppose that's another reason I make art. It's a form of love, one that is based on beauty and in the present. I don't think I've ever loved in the way people with deep, romantic relationships do. Such love is tiring—I feel like it would drain the spirit."

"But what do you know of love?" Cezal asked.

She gave a light laugh. "Well, you'd be surprised—don't assume so quickly I've always been this way. I know enough to know what I want and don't want. Though admittedly, it's all very abstract to me. It used to pain me that I never experienced it, at least in the way I hoped I would. I felt like I was missing out, and it gave me deep despair because I didn't know what to live for. But I've gotten used to it. I've accepted it, and I don't think it's worth the emotional pain to reopen that part of myself."

"So you think you've cut a part of yourself off?"

"I suppose so. It's still there, but I push it down."

"Do you think that's healthy?" Cezal asked.

She gave a wry smile. "Healthy, I don't know. It just is. I suppose it's a part of me that will always be there. It's a very tender part, one that I protect like I would a child."

"Is it worth it?" Cezal asked, looking up at the ceiling, trying to make his tone sound as inoffensive as possible.

"Suppressing that part of myself?' Alja asked.

"Yes."

"Oh, Cezal, is anything worth it? I'm just trying my best to make do. That's how it goes."

The train rocked a bit as it went through a curve, and by then, it was getting dimmer outside. The trees passed as they always did and were wonderful as they always were, covered in snow, glimmering in the muted, early evening light.

"This is perhaps a rather out-there idea," Cezal said, still staring at the ceiling, "but seeing as to how you're getting off the train the day after tomorrow and I have nowhere in Sectohal I need to be in particular, what if we stayed together for a while? Perhaps just a month or so while you do your art."

Alja looked over at him. "That's rather abrupt. But I suppose I don't see why not. It is pretty isolated there, and it is winter, so it would be nice not to be alone when it's so dark and dreary."

"Yes. And then I can continue onto Briedavga afterward. It will be interesting to get some insight into the artistic process," Cezal added with a smile.

"Yes, I suppose so," replied Alja, looking again out the window with a small smile.

10

———

Alja's family home was constructed almost entirely of wood and, by the looks of it, hadn't been repaired since she was a child. The snow spread itself over the ground and collected in clumps on the trees and rocks. The sky by this time was almost always enveloped by the gray haze of winter. It was a three-hour walk from the train stop to get to the cabin, much of it over snow-covered, sparsely marked footpaths that wound seemingly directionless through the trees. The air, however, was of a crispness that Cezal hadn't enjoyed for quite some time, and he felt like a damp, nearly mildewed rag that had just been left outside in the breeze to finally dry.

Alja and Cezal wore leather boots. She was bedecked with fine, pine martin furs, while Cezal donned a woolen shirt and pants over his standard canvas ones. It was near when the world was becoming noticeably dimmer in preparation for the night, that, through the dreariness, they finally got to the cabin. It itself was constructed entirely of wood, with worn, sky blue paint to accent the gables and other features of its façade. Alja dragged the wooden door over the thin layer of snow, and they stepped in, Alja taking a deep breath as the musty smell of wood filled her nostrils.

Later that night, after they started and were eating a dinner of rye pancakes and stale coffee with a smokey aftertaste, they got to unwinding from the long day.

"Do you know why it was that I enjoyed talking to you at first, Cezal?" Alja asked, the light from the fire flickering over her face.

He shook his head. "No, I don't."

"I could tell that you were a person who didn't live for anyone else."

He nodded absently. "Hm, I suppose you're right. I don't, but I don't know if that's necessarily a good thing."

She shrugged. "Yes, I know, but it's hard to find people who don't live for the sake of others. To go from the point of living for no one to living for something or for some good reason is an easier step than the leap from no longer living for the sake of others to living for something valuable."

"And why is that so important to you?" he asked. "Not living for others."

She spoke, looking into the fire. "It's something I have to consider more, but I think it's because it irritates me to no end to see people live for the sake of others. It feels so weak and unbecoming. That said, I know we all have that potential to stray from the path we want to make for ourselves, myself included, so I wanted to be, I think, with someone who would help me retain that part of me, lest I too start to live for others. It probably would have been wiser to have sought out a person who was living for *something*, thinking back on it, as opposed to someone who was aimlessly floating through life, such as you seem to. Ah, but it's good that it's come to be this way, I've decided. This way, perhaps we can learn and grow together. Wouldn't you say?"

"Hm, yes, one could even say it's nicer that way. But what

do you think is better to live for?" Cezal asked.

She took a bite of the pancakes and washed it down with a sip of coffee. "Oh, it's different for everybody. I don't know. For me, it is my art and interior world. For you? I don't know. It seems that you're trying to figure that out in your own roundabout way, wouldn't you say?"

He thought for a moment. She noticed the light from the stove fire flickering on his face. "I suppose so. I suppose I have a somewhat contented dissatisfaction with my life so far, as much of an oxymoron as that may be. I'm okay with my past and choices I've made but I don't want to live that way anymore."

They sat in silence for a while, sitting back at opposite sides of the smallish table looking into the stove fire. The sound of flames flickering and frigid wind made the house creak and settle. "I must say," began Cezal, "it sounds like a rather lonely existence, to live for your interior world, wouldn't you say?"

"I can see how it seems that way." She smiled. "And I do think I'm a rather lonely, dissatisfied person, but I've come largely to accept that part of myself." She stopped herself for a second. "But I should be clear. It is not just I who inhabits my interior world. No, in fact, there are a great many people I've made up who live there too—in some cases different parts of myself I've tried to make into full people and in other cases simply different people altogether. And they help me feel less alone."

Cezal raised his eyebrows. "How do you mean?"

"I mean when I'm in my interior world, I think of them, and when I'm laying down or even just staring into the distance, I'll imagine they're with me, and I can interact with them as I would anybody else in the real world. We have coffee dates, watch the sunset together, get into fights, and there are even some who die or move away, only to visit once a year or so."

Cezal looked at her rather in a surprised way. "Well, that's quite something. I don't know what to make of that."

She smiled a bit. "Well, there's nothing really to make of it. It's how I've come to be in the world. I know it sounds rather strange, but when that's been the reality of your life for a while, one comes to habituate oneself to it. There's one person in particular whom I've been spending a lot of time with recently. Her name's Malanta, and she is the sunshine of my world. She's my daughter."

Cezal's eyes widened. "What do you mean your daughter?"

She laughed lightly. "Yes. Please, don't seem so startled by this. You act that way and make me feel as though it's some deep, dark secret to keep hidden. I know it's unconventional, but I promise I'm not crazy."

"Yes, yes, no, I didn't mean to seem all that surprised." Cezal stammered. "Certainly, you can see why I wouldn't have been expecting you to say Malanta is your daughter, but no, please feel free to continue."

She smiled. "Well, it's just that. I know it's not like *actually* having a child. She only exists when it's convenient for me. But it's nice. I think it's important that people be around kids. They help keep one young. I know my inclinations and how much I withdraw from the outer world, but to have a wonderful daughter in my interior world gives it a certain, special glow. I have someone special to look forward to seeing. I get to be there for someone. It's different than my friends there—they don't need me in the same way. It's more that we enjoy each other's company. And my daughter doesn't have to grow up either.

"Sometimes she's a teenager, and I get to give her advice on friendship or relationship drama, and other times she's a young adult trying to find her place in the world, or even a new parent, and I get to be something of a grandma for that time. But usually, she's five-and-three-fourths, as she's always sure to remind everybody when they ask her age. It's a golden time. It really is. She's a very curious girl, and she loves to explore the world. It's so nice to have someone to show the world to, you know—someone for whom it's still full of wonder." Alja smiled and looked into the fire. "It really is a very beautiful thing. She brings me joy, Cezal. Perhaps you can meet her some time—once you've gotten more used to the idea, that is."

* * *

A couple of days later, as they were preparing more pancakes for dinner and Alja brought in more wood for the fire, Cezal looked around for some potatoes or onions.

"I hope the concept of Malanta isn't too unsettling for you. I—" She paused, walking over to Cezal in the kitchen area. "You know, there's almost always a reason people are the way they are. And if there's one thing I've learned about people is they're usually afraid. I have to remind myself of that often to keep myself from resenting them too much. I don't say that to imply that you're afraid, but rather that I'm afraid. The bad that people see in the world is usually related to the bad they see in themselves. My mom used to tell me that's what draws people to the concept of purity. 'They exalt this empty idea because,' she would say with vigor, 'they see the lack of purity in themselves and hope that by worshipping it, they'll get rid of the evil and vileness they have cultivated in their own spirit.' I'm sure you can already tell, but that never works. That, too, is why people are afraid of some ideas. They censor themselves and put faux barriers up in the name of their purity. Some of the more closed-off of them even worry about ideas that will corrupt the minds of the youth and fail to see the irony in that fear."

Cezal found a few potatoes and nodded, still looking for onions. "It's interesting you bring it up," he said. "Zamen had some very similar feelings on the subject. Of course, though, nonetheless, he intended to cultivate a purity culture in his town."

Alja shook her head. "I resent them—such people—both the ideologues and those who fall prey to it. I left my town in part because it was filled with them. They did it with such moral arrogance, too, looking down upon all the heretics of the world, looking down upon all those who dare to live their life. Such people, they are a sham—a great gilded chest made of rotten wood and filled with nothing but their own vacuousness. And that is a great irony. They look for the rot in other people because they are too afraid to face the rot in themselves. That is why they are weak. That is why they must proclaim the rest of the world impure. One shouldn't trust them—they are people to avoid. I think in many ways, my mom wanted to see me live a life she wasn't able to, which is why she placed so much emphasis on this point. But yes, the worst parts of all the world lie within. That's what people forget. All the evil they see outside of them lies in the heart. That's the only place it's ever been. But anyhow, I suppose I'm rambling at this point."

Cezal began cutting up the potatoes after giving up on finding the onions. "That's an interesting idea," he said, looking down at the knife to make sure he wouldn't cut his fingers as he chopped. "It sounds like you were around a lot of unhappy people."

Alja smiled lightly. "Well I did tell you there's always a reason everyone is the way they are." She looked to Cezal to see his reaction. He just grunted and kept chopping. "But there are other things that it seems like more and more people do."

"Hm?" offered Cezal.

Alja pulled up a chair next to him and began to explain, crossing her legs in a comfortable position. "It seems more and more that people think of themselves as the object of the world. They engage with that in which they shouldn't engage—namely harmful narratives they should simply reject instead of complaining about. Even look at the fact that we have ideologues in the first place. Their followers will constantly be let down. All I hear is them complaining about their problems and self-perceived shortcomings. The irony is that many agree with me, especially those who are older and look upon the youth with a hardened eye no longer as perceptive as it used to be. Ah, but they too view the world as working in a certain way, and we are all the object of whatever grand system they hold dear and bought into their whole lives without even realizing it. They forget that all the world, all the civilization, all the ideas we have, and the systems we uphold with them are only there because we uphold them. Not because there is anything more or less inherently legitimate about it. They fall prey to the same dynamics that the younger generations do. They just interpreted them in a different way. People have forgotten that there is no higher truth, no reality that eludes them. As such, there's no aspect of the modern world that cannot come to be understood and changed."

She stopped a bit, and Cezal looked over to make sure she was still there. She was watching him chop.

"I think most people will come to regret their lives."

"Yeah?" Cezal asked.

"Yes. I think so."

"Why so?"

"Because they think they understand that which they don't."

* * *

The cool night breeze gently moved the lace curtains in the window that overlooked the ocean, and Alja awoke and stepped outside barefoot in a white nightgown that moved in the breeze in the same way as the bedroom curtain. The moon, nestled among the stars, hung in the sky, having waned almost to a sliver that nonetheless shed enough light to drape over the seaside. A short figure, dressed in well-cleaned rags, stood between some orange trees in the distance. The smell of the sea mixed with that of orange oil. Alja looked to the figure and then to the sea. When she looked back at the figure, an old woman, a grandmotherly sort with kind eyes was standing before her, only a bit more than an arm's length away.

"Good evening, Lemantin," Alja said. "It's been quite a while since I've seen you. I thought you were dead."

"Well, I've been away for a while." she answered, the moonlight drifting off her eyes. Shades of shadow danced across the rest of her face.

"Oh," replied Alja. "What brings you here?"

Lemantin shrugged her shoulders as well as she could, being as hunched over as she was. "It seemed the right time to come and speak with you."

"Oh?" replied Alja, raising her eyebrows. "Please do."

"You are slipping, my dear. I can see it shining through—the way you look in the mirror, the way you look at your spoon as you use it to eat."

There were at the cliff, the tall grass blowing in the warm sea breeze. The ocean churned below, a deep blue immensity.

"Do you hear the waves, Alja?"

"Yes."

"Do you see them?"

Alja looked down into the molten blue and the electric crack and began to feel the current. Back and forth. She inhaled and exhaled.

"Be careful when you look into it. You will think you're there, but you're still standing above it. Listen to the birds chirping, my dear. Do you hear them? They've just woken up in the early morning. Do you smell the citrus?"

She heard the birds and their crisp cries that fill the world again with life. She inhaled deeply and smelled the oranges.

"You're living on the frontier of this world and another one. One is the real, and the other is a simulation of the real. Be careful."

The wind began to pick up and the waves grew louder. Alja watched the birds fly out of the trees in droves, speckling the early morning sky with the sounds of their wings. What a crisp morning.

And she felt the current pick up and drag her back and forth until the air felt wet, and she couldn't breathe any longer. Back and forth. Back and forth. The air was no longer a problem, nor was the cold. Because it was okay to suffocate, and it was okay to freeze. Back and forth. Back and forth.

One night after dinner, Alja and Cezal were sitting down near the fire with hot water. There was a storm outside, and Alja had gone out to walk in it. She was out about five minutes before coming back in again. By then, Cezal was already at the fire.

"And how was it outside?" he asked as she was putting the wood plank in place to lock the door.

She smiled. "Cold. But it's nice to feel the chill in your bones every once in a while. And of course, storms have their own particular beauty."

She got some hot water too and sat down. They both stared into the fire for some time. They talked of logistics and how they would get more food for the coming weeks. The rye was running rather low, and Cezal didn't have much more dried meat. They decided to venture to the closest village, a three-hour's-walk there and back, to get more food and to buy a proper coat for Cezal. Briedavga was rather cold and wet, so his wool wouldn't do.

As often happens when the night wears on, they got to matters of the heart. Alja sat lounging on the couch, her feet still on the ground, but the rest of her half leaning against the backrest and half laying on the seat. It was the only cushioned piece of furniture in the house—a parting gift from the carpenter in town with whom her father had frequently spent his nights—and Cezal sat on a wooden chair, worn but well-crafted. Both pieces of furniture were facing the box stove in the middle of the room, the door to which Alja had left slightly ajar to allow for some light to dance about the cabin.

"I've come to see that people don't want me, at least deep down, they don't," Alja began. "And that's okay. They don't have to. It is hard for me not to resent humanity sometimes. It still hurts… Don't take this as having veiled meaning that I'm trying to apply to you—when I say *humanity* I do mean humanity."

"Ah," Cezal replied, looking into the fire. He turned his head. "Why do you think that is?"

Alja shrugged her shoulders and pursed her lips a bit. "I don't know. I know, on a conscious level, it's probably self-inflicted. It's not as though there would be some kind of grand conspiracy against me… Throughout my life, though, I've always thought myself unwelcome. Perhaps you'd think that's rather self-important." She cleared her throat. "Well, I suppose it is on some level, but that's how I felt. It's weird how that feeling follows you around. The scope expands and contracts. Sometimes, it felt like I was unwelcome to live, and sometimes it just felt like I was unwelcome among those around me."

Cazal tried to make an empathetic nod to show he was engaged. She kept staring into the fire.

"There's a strange legitimacy to unwelcomeness. It's exclusion, yes, but unwelcomeness is exclusion backed by moral justification, or at least it feels that way. Then your mere *existence* becomes the moral violation. In all honesty, I don't really know how to get through it. Because I don't want to live this way. I used to talk about it more, but you're the first one in many years whom I've told this to. I keep to myself mostly because, well, aside from that, it puts you in a rather vulnerable position. You can tell by the way someone speaks they don't understand most of the time. They'll usually try to tell you something that makes you feel better, but they do this awkwardly, like a foal just after birth, still learning to walk. The effort is nice, but they say it out of a sense of duty, or in trying to prove themselves, or even out of thinking they can commiserate, figuring that's what you want. But really, it just comes off as out of touch. And who can blame them? I do appreciate their effort. And as well, you don't want to elaborate too much on how you feel, because that would be rather self-absorbed, wouldn't it? There a plenty of people with bigger, *more real*, problems, wouldn't you say? So you have a pit of isolation as a consolation prize for reaching out."

She stopped and looked out the window into the night. "Of course, anything having to do with a relationship goes both ways, so I must be to blame too, at least in part. So then I have to ask, do I really want to feel better if I don't do what I can to get out of it? Maybe so. Does that mean you don't have the justification for feeling bad about yourself? I suppose not, though I suppose really one doesn't need a justification to feel any emotion. But in either case," she added flatly, "it doesn't really help to feel bad about yourself. But there is something about self-pity that is attractive, comforting even. Maybe that's why I tend toward it so much. But as for a value statement on the issue of unwantedness? I don't know. If I'm being unkind with myself, then I'll say there's no validity to my sadness. Oh, but it's so lonely, and nobody really cares anyways as long as you stay out of their way, right?" She lifted her head to look at Cezal. "Right?"

He turned his head to face her, his eyes soft. "Are you looking for an actual answer from me?"

She continued looking at him for a second. "No," She sighed. "Not really… But anyhow, I know it's self-important to care so much about myself—guilt and sadness and all that are rather arrogant emotions. I guess they all sort of are, aren't they? That too was rhetorical, by the way," she added with a light chuckle.

"And I suppose if I'm being completely honest, Cezal, I think I wouldn't know what to do with myself if I were happy. I know how I am, and I know myself well enough to see the cycles that I operate off of—the sadness, and depressive feelings, and hopelessness, and then the despair that gives way to a new day; the reborn realization that my life is mine to live. And when I'm in that upswing, I think, what a tired theme it is: all that melancholy, all that sadness, but I go back to it one way or another, and sometimes, when in my episodes of despair, I think about hope and happiness, and I deride them and wish them away. Why? Half because I feel bound to the cycle and want something dramatic to happen to break myself out of it, and half because, as I said before, I don't know what else I'd do." She shifted to an upright position and sat leaning toward the fire, her elbows resting on her knees.

"But I've contemplated it before. I think the people may look at melancholy and disappointment as being superficial. The one's you can't really have deep discussions with, but who are rather more inclined to talk about their vegetable gardens or the ailment of their knee, or, among the intelligentsia, their propensity to talk about politics in the same way one would talk about a football game—they're missing the point of those who like nostalgia. They don't see the value it can give… Ah, but to their credit, it has its place, sure, but it too gets tiring after a while. And who am I to say such unaware people aren't often happier than those like me?"

They sat in silence for some time, listening to the crackle of the fire. Cezal didn't know how to respond, though, of course, nor did Alja expect him to.

"I suppose I'm tired of my life. It's just tiring. I guess that's why some people sell it all to travel the world. Not entirely unlike what you're doing. But even that leaves one unfulfilled after a while. It's just a distraction in the end. A distraction from what, I don't know."

The sound of the fire filled the room, punctuated by the lyricism of the damp wind outside.

"Perhaps," she mused, "it's the value that we seek—meaning." She scoffed. "Oh, what a word. What a word it is. And what if I lived my life trying to find meaning?" She shook her head. "No, 'create' would be the better word there. But I don't know Cezal. Suppose I did do that, then what? What am I trying to make this meaning for? Eh? At least nostalgia lets you bask in the rose-colored past. I suppose that's a kind of meaning. But maybe, Cezal, just maybe, it's all a distraction."

The wind outside started to pick up, and the house began creaking more.

"Maybe so," replied Cezal. "I can't claim to have much any more insight than you." And they stared out the window for a while at what little of the outside storm they could see.

"People seem to talk a lot about joining something bigger than oneself—a mission of some sorts, an overarching life goal, or even a religion. Have you thought of that?" Cezal broke in.

Alja looked at him, coolly engaging with his proposition, and then lowered her head again to talk.

"There's some merit in those points, yes. Say you were to join some religion that told you there *is* meaning, whatever that may be, and you bought into it with your entire being. Is that not still just a distraction?"

Cezal shook his head. "I don't know."

"When you come to consider it," Alja began again, "the proposition almost makes you question human development itself. These questions we're asking aren't the ones you ask yourself when you're just trying to survive, when you need to find water, or make a fire, or even get over some ailment or another. At such times, it falls by the wayside. But we strive to overcome these petty struggles to get steadiness, to get security. And for what? Then you really have to face yourself. I don't know. I think it's a possibility for enough of humanity to collectively manage to become self-aware enough to break out of the cycles of history. We're a way off from that, I think, but at some point or another, we'll be in a golden age for at least long enough to think we've broken out. But if we do, we'll just be forced to face ourselves in a different way.

"If that happens long enough, you almost wonder if humanity will fade into existence—slowly die off. Not some dramatic mass extinction, but simply people deciding not to eat anymore or not have kids or simply kill themselves in one fell swoop. Why? Because what's keeping them here? They will have 'won,' at that point.

"But I'm rambling. Yes, there's merit to joining something bigger than yourself, but it's just another distraction at the end of the day." She smiled a bit. "Ah, but perhaps there will come a day when I'm tired of wandering in the tundra of stunted lives and half-cultivated meaning. Maybe I'll buy into distraction. Maybe that's all you can ask for. I suppose that's the value of ideology."

They sat in silence for some time.

"I know this reflects rather poorly on me... It's a very weak person who feels as I do. It's a rejection of meaning, I suppose. It's a very unbecoming thing to suggest when you understand my reasoning because in my reasoning, you see what I don't consider; what I take for granted. And so it's a point of deep shame. But I feel it nonetheless, and I think most who would deride me are themselves little better much of the time. It's not as though they would have acted differently if they had been in my shoes or I in theirs. At least, I suppose, I know I'm sick. I know I'm detestable."

He turned to look at her and watched the fire flicker in her eyes.

* * *

The midmorning sunlight flowed through the window and cast itself nicely across the rickety, wooden table. Better years that table had seen. But it was old, and so it had seen much. The boards that made it up were splintered and worn from use. Many stains adorned the perimeter, like ghosts of a livelier past. Alja was boiling coffee, and Cezal was making more rye pancakes.

"You don't seem to be too receptive of Malanta, Cezal. Do you have a problem with her?"

He looked up, eyebrows raised. "Well…" he began, "I suppose not, but you have to admit, it's a rather strange concept, pretending this person exists. I don't know. I'll keep an open mind, yes, but it's really quite weird."

"She can be a real person, though, Cezal. And if you're avoiding it, it's just because you find the idea of her weird, don't you think that's not a horribly valid reason for rejecting something?"

"Well, I don't know about the first part, but yes, I agree with you. I said I'm keeping an open mind."

Alja left the pot on the stove and came to sit facing Cezal. "My point is you should be actively confronting the strangeness you feel when thinking of Malanta. She's really quite nice, Cezal. She's young and full of life. She's like a ray of sunshine. I haven't felt this way in quite a while. It could do you some good to have her energy rub off on you."

"Ehh," Cezal wavered, "well yes, I suppose so."

"Oh, come now, Cezal. There's no need to squirm. Come on, talk to her." Alja spoke those words not out of annoyance but rather as gentle prodding, the way one would prod a child to say hello to a playmate. He looked to the left, by the washbasin.

"Hi, Malanta. How are you?"

"No, no," interrupted Alja, waving her hand. "Malanta isn't over there. She's not some invisible being. Look into her eyes when you speak to her. Look into my eyes. Speak to me. Of course, though, I am not she, and nor do I look like her. I have talked with you before about what Malanta looks like—so loveable and filled with sunshine. Talk to her as you would any five-year-old. She's very curious about the world. I'm sure she would love to discover the stars with you, to take walks into the forest, watch you make food. She's a wonderful child, Cezal, she really is."

He took a deep breath and did his best to resist his desire to recoil. "Hi Malanta, how are you doing this morning?" he asked Alja.

"Wow, you're not used to kids, are you?" said Alja with a kind smile.

Cezal stared blankly back at her.

"Oh, don't take yourself so seriously. Thank you for trying."

A moment later.

"I'm good," replied Malanta.

There was stilted conversation back in forth for a few minutes, but after some time, a smile crept over Cezal's face as he began to see the child. "You know, Malanta," he said, "back in my town way far away, there were many children perhaps a bit older than you are who used to play outside on the streets with a ball—"

"What happened to them?" Malanta asked.

Cezal laughed. "Oh nothing, they're probably still there. It used to feel like they would never grow up. There were always children there. Now *that's* when you start to feel old when the children seem frozen in time, and every summer, you think of how small they all are."

"I'm not small."

"No, I know that," replied Cezal with a warm smile. "I don't know any kids in this area, but I can carve a ball for you to play with, and we could play with it together. Would that be fun?"

And in Malanta, a wonderful dandelion of a smile bloomed inside of her. "Mmhmm, that sounds fun!"

* * *

Alja and Cezal often took walks in the forest and enjoyed the pine trees and the snow, fluffy and white. It was not overly dry, but rather gathered on the branches in small piles and stuck delightfully onto the bark of the trees. The sound of the forest when there wasn't any wind was deafening in its silence. One would pause to listen to that silence, only to become aware of one's own breath and heartbeat. Then, a breeze became again and the sound of needles brushing together and snow falling filled the air, like pollen from a tree in spring.

They trudged together for some time. The sun, for the first time in nearly two weeks, was visible. Suddenly Alja stopped and turned to face Cezal. "You know," she began, "we all thought my grandpa—the one who owned the farm—was crazy in his later years. Not a true craziness. Perhaps 'absently eccentric' would be the better term to use. He seemed quite sharp in his vacantness if that makes sense. He used to sit out on the front porch for hours at a time in a wooden rocking chair, the same as the one I've told you about before, looking out onto the dry, empty fields. He'd have no drink, no book, no nap—nothing but him and the chair, looking out, again, in that absent awareness. I came out there one day, only a few months before he died and asked him what he looked at when he was outside.

"He didn't answer immediately. By that time, he was, of course, well past the age when one feels the urgency to speak. I didn't know when he would answer, so I just pulled up another chair and sat next to him, looking out into the fields too, feeling the scorching sun on my skin. It was rather depressing, though I've always found the heat depressing. But finally, he broke the silence and told me with his voice creaky from age and disuse, that after you've been around long enough, the sun is golden.

"When I was younger," Alja continued explaining, "I thought he was purposefully trying to be cryptic when he used to say stuff like that, but as I get older, I realize he just didn't care that much about being understood. At the time though, I asked what he meant—how could the sun be golden?

"His reply was to instruct me to look out at the land. He told me that it's barren and dead, but that it used to be lush and well-tended, filled with life. It was his land, and he had taken pride in it. He was disappointed that those barren fields were all he was going to leave us." Cezal stood there listening to her story with his hands on his hips. "His whole life had played out there, on those fields. I remember looking out at the land he was referring to. It was as dry and dead as ever. Dirt and dust with a few weeds growing here and there. But then I remember he looked directly at me with surprising presence and told me that despite all that, the sun was still there, and it had been there long before I came and would be there long after I'm gone. And that it is golden—that seemed to be an important point to him. After he said this, I remember him smiling a bit." And Alja herself smiled as she recounted the scene. "Then he told me that he thought I'd see it too someday. I remember thinking again that it was one of those senile, half-in-this-world-half-in-another kinds of things, and didn't take what he said to heart, other than interpreting it as carrying the solemn sentiment observed in those of their later years."

She stopped to take a deep breath and watched the condensation billow up into the air as she exhaled. She and Cezal both stood facing each other foot-deep in snow, pine trees on both sides of them, extending indefinitely in both directions.

"And you know, Cezal, I think I do see it now since getting to the cabin. The sun *is* golden, or at least, it can be." She sighed. "And I'm tired, Cezal. I'm tired. That's why I think I'll go. Maybe not for good, but for a little while… I think it may be good for you to go too, to go to the city."

Cezal shook his head. "Hold on, what do you mean? All the sudden? What are y—"

She shook her head in turn. "Cezal, don't get all hot and bothered by this. Nothing's happening right now. But you need to get on with your life, don't you think?"

He took a deep breath and raised both of his eyebrows. "I… I suppose so. But… I don't know. Do I really need to go right now? What is with the sudden change-of-heart?"

She shook her head again. "Cezal, please. What really are you even doing here in the first place? Let's be honest with ourselves. Are you just giving up to complacency? There *is* more. You may think I'm hinting that I've given up, but I haven't, Cezal. But I'm also not you, and you have a goal, as nebulous as it is. And so it's important that you pursue it."

He paused and looked at her for a second. She looked at him, her expression not hardened, but unchanging.

"I suppose you're right," he finally said. "But still, why do you bring this up now?"

She looked at him, somewhat perplexed. "It's no sudden change of heart. I didn't think what I was saying was so unexpected. Yes, I brought it up abruptly, but I didn't intend it to be a revelation. Don't take what I say the wrong way." She started walking again and looked back at Cezal. "Shall we continue?"

"Yes," he said absentmindedly. "But will you stay here? What is your plan?"

She kept walking and looking forward as she talked. "I don't know. We'll see. I don't think I'll stay for too much longer at the cabin after you leave. I suppose I've come to see I'm not going to accept my dissatisfaction any longer. I may simply be wanting to move in a vain attempt to avoid it, but I think I need to go back to my own house and make a real life for myself there." She stopped walking and turned to face Cezal. "How I'll do that, I don't know, but I'll figure it out. The emptiness of life is, at times, deafening. I think the thought of my existence is a pain because I feel at some times that I do not understand it, and at other times, I don't think there is anything to understand. And so there's a heavy abyss of emptiness that claws at me from inside. And I'm tired of it. I don't think there's more."

* * *

Later that night, once they got back, there was a storm that rocked the house and gave the world an unsettling flair. Cezal was glad they had brought in extra wood. They sat around the fire as they did most nights, and the flames flickered, and the windows rattled.

"When I was a kid," Alja said as she lounged on the couch, "my mom used to tell me lots of stories to help me get to sleep, or, on quiet afternoons, just to keep me occupied when I was bored of playing on my own. There's one story I remember that is apt for our situation. You may think I'm implying something about you in this story, and there's an extent to which I am, but don't take it to heart. It's more just a general lesson that's good for anyone, including myself, to hear."

"Okay," replied Cezal with the masked trepidation that would come from any vague disclaimer for what would likely amount to a rather biting metaphor.

"Well," began Alja, "she told me a story about a boy, perhaps sixteen years old or so who lived near us many years ago, when my mom was herself a child. He was rather sickly and often complained that he felt like the world was against him. He was the kind of person who is negative and doesn't see how their words and energy suck the vitality out of those around them. Well, this boy had reason to feel like the world was against him, she told me. His shoes seemed to get holes in them more often than the others, he got sick more often than the others, and when he was younger, his caregivers seemed to be harder on him than on the others. It was like this for a while, and so he adopted this view of himself. His attitude deepened, and he continued to see himself as subject to the whim of a faceless, unfair world—the outsider to his own life. This went on as it usually did, and people didn't particularly like him because of his constant lamenting, but they put up with him. One day though, when he was cutting a tree down, working up a sweat, and looking forward to lunch, he suddenly vanished, his ax hitting the ground with a dull thud. In a split second, he was in the middle of a cold, green expanse with rolling hills that extended seemingly indefinitely in all directions.

"It was nearly dusk, and the cold was damp and biting. He stood up and looked around, but none of it seemed at all familiar. There was no wind, but rather a wet fog that draped itself over the hills and made it look like it would rain any-time. There was only a deep green, thick, moplike grass and clusters of wild, white daffodils with happy, yellow centers. The boy, very disoriented, stood there for some time in shock. He did his best to look for a higher point to try and get his bearings. All the hills, however, were roughly the same height, so he kept walking forward. The strange thing is that it never got brighter or darker. It never started to rain. It was sim-ply the same—the perpetual dusk and withholding sky. He couldn't tell how long he had been walking, but it felt to him like many days. He did what he could to get water, licking the dew off the grass, but it only went so far, and he really began to feel the thirst after some time. And so eventually, he finally lost hope and sat on the hill and began to cry. He knew his situation was helpless. By then, he was sure he was no longer on any earthly land but rather some other world where there was only cold grass and a foreboding sky.

"Just as he began to truly sob, it started to rain, and it rained so thickly he was able to cup his hands and collect lots of water. He was reinvigorated and was full of an elation he had seldom felt before. Never mind that his clothes were soaked through, and he had no food. All that could wait because he had water, and he was living in the ecstasy of the moment. He felt much better once he was able to quench his thirst, but of course, then he was very wet and still very hungry, so he wasn't able to keep warm anymore. He ended up freezing to death a few hours later, cursing his existence as his teeth chattered away."

Cezal looked at Alja, eyes widened. "That's quite the story. A bit brutal for a young child, though, don't you think?"

She nodded. "I can certainly see how you'd think that. But this wasn't some story my mother told to get me to stop complaining about my chores. Rather, it was a story intended to get you to see that you make your world, and your actions have long-term causes. You see, in her day, people believed that there existed a deep, pervasive justice. They told such stories in order to teach us about this justice. Of course, it's a simplified parable. In reality, people don't get banished to the grasslands. Instead, they slowly build it into their own lives. Regardless, she expected me to learn from his example, and indeed, I do think there's a fair deal of value I've learned from her story."

He thought for a few moments. "I still don't really get the moral. It sounds like they're just telling you to accept your lot in life. If you complain too much, then one day you'll randomly disappear to some corner of the earth, then you'll *really* be sorry."

She smiled and shook her head. "There's more to it than that, Cezal. It's a story to say that you determine your reality. This is not to say that if you're starving, you should simply have positive thinking. No, it would be highly improper to consider this story in such simplistic terms. It has to do with what you think your relationship with the world is and how you exist within that context."

Cezal furrowed his eyebrows. "If you say so."

The fire was fierce, and the flames danced accordingly, swaying with the shadows that cast themselves over the walls. Back and forth, they went. Back and forth.

* * *

It was dark, and the fire was barely embers. Alja lay on her bedroll atop some bundled straw and stared at the ceiling, the rafters crossing her field of view, casting a shadow on the space above them. *And what is possession?* Silence rang through the air. Even the wind had stopped. *I can almost hold it. Hold onto the moment. Oh, to break free. To dredge myself out.* Back and forth, the world flowed. *That would be something—then you could look upon the infinite smallness of your lifespan and see it for what it is. That would make you take stock of it all, wouldn't it?*

Ah, but I guess you can never have a moment.

She closed her eyes and rolled to her side. Back and forth, she flowed.

I guess you can never have anything, really.

Eventually, the world clawed into her long enough that sleep was able to take over.

11

———

Gray filled the sky: deeply and fully. The morning light trickled in, dully illuminating the cabin.

Alja sat up from her bedroll. Cezal was still lying down on his.

"You know, Cezal, I've noticed more and more that there is something inside of me that often tries to claw itself out. It's a part of myself that tries to break out of my own skin, as though my body were a tight sack suffocating it." Her eyebrows were furrowed, and she looked with intensity at a pebble on the floor. "It's a primal part of me that needs to live. I don't know where it comes from or why I have it…" She shook her head. "Perhaps I made it up, like I made up Malanta, to be a counter to the other parts of myself. Though this part of me, if I did make it up, came about far more organically than did Malanta—far more subconsciously. If anything, that part of me is more original, and the *I* that I usually am is the mental creation of that part of me yearning to explode with life. It's a part of me that I feel has existed before *Alja* ever did. It's funny to think about, you know, what I could make of that part of me." She looked at Cezal. "I could embrace it. I often wonder what it would be like to do so. I don't know. Perhaps it would consume me—consume *this* I. Ah, but what am I doing, speaking as though I were *real*!" She smiled at Cezal, and he did his best to smile back. "Yes, I suppose then, we're really one in the same—the different parts of me, that is. Ah, but it's so strange a sensation to feel as though you're losing your grip on reality, like a balloon whose string is slipping through your hands as it floats away into the blue skies. What happens when the string runs out? I don't know, but it's not good to repress oneself, wouldn't you say? Perhaps I'll embrace it a bit when I feel it coming on. I should get to know *that* me more; I've shut her out of my life for far too long."

* * *

The cabin was dusty. Cezal was on the floor, and light filtered through the windows, the particulates in the air shining under the shafts of sunlight.

Can you feel the dust on your skin, Cezal? Can you feel it in your lungs? Breathe deeply. Embrace it.

He sat with Alja by the fire. It was evening again. "I don't see how it can possibly be worth it in the end," she told him, her eyes not breaking from the fire's glow. "We're falling through existence. There's no greater purpose we serve, wouldn't you say? And so we have our emotions and our relationships for comfort. We have love." She nodded. "Yes, that's what we have, and we shouldn't underestimate it even if it's not always enough." She raised her finger at Cezal in preparation for this last point. "But that said, neither can brutality. Because until people are tired, brutality doesn't stop. And until it stops, it will win. And what's done is done, Cezal." She closed her eyes and shook her head. "And there's no making up for it. But it's all so cyclical." She looked through the musty air to find his eyes. "Yes, we will overcome brutality, but then people will once again succumb to it. Because that's the way things go. People take peace for granted. They say things that feel nice and liberating in the moment and don't realize how good they have it. They don't realize they slander all that is right in the world. And they will invariably pay the price. And it's tiring, Cezal. I know I have been that slanderer before—we all have at some time or another. But that doesn't make it better or okay. And after a time of brutality, when once again we are reminded of the importance of peace and love and understanding, how does that help those who have been killed and maimed already? Hm?"

Cezal began to answer.

"No, no, Cezal, it was a rhetorical question. How does that make it better? That is why there is no real justice in the world. And I can't help but look at it all, Cezal, and ask, 'Is it worth it?' Because how could it be? We are all falling through existence. All of life is simply a rather peculiar iteration of the dissipation of energy. So how can it be worth it?"

The snow fell heavier outside, muffling the world.

She took a deep breath. "Yes. I sometimes think about the so-called end of history, when all the energy in the universe has spread out and when there can no longer be any life. When it's all simply dark and cold, and then it'll finally be over, there can be no more suffering then. There will be no one to hurt or be hurt."

"Yes," Cezal answered hesitantly, "but nor will there be love and life and happiness."

She turned to look at him. "What is love and happiness to brutality? Huh? What hollow comfort that provides for those who suffer."

"But is it not often that those who truly suffer are the ones who appreciate love and happiness the most?"

"Yes, I suppose so." She sniffed.

"And suppose there was some person who bore such suffering and decided that it was worth it. What then?"

She raised an eyebrow. "What do you mean what then?"

He shrugged cautiously. "Would you be able to uphold what you've said before about life not being worth it?"

She paused for some time, and Cezal again looked out the window—more snow, though of course, he couldn't tell because it was so dark out. "I suppose not. Perhaps then one can only make that decision individually. But the dead don't miss happiness or feel sad. They simply don't exist, so what does it matter?"

"You say that you can't make up for the bad that has happened in the past, but can you 'make up' for the good that has happened in the past either?"

The fire cracked loudly.

"Well, no," she replied. "But they don't cancel each other out either. And the bad is unjustifiable, so one comes to the conclusion…" She trailed off and stared into the fire.

"What conclusion?" he asked.

"The conclusion that it would be better if there were no life."

His voice felt heavy. "Oh. That's a harsh conclusion."

"Yes, I know. But I think it's true."

"Perhaps it is." Another look to the window. The floor was cold.

"Yes, indeed, indeed. But I don't know." She shook her head. "I can't claim to be so wise or knowing. Of course, I can only speak to my personal experience. I suppose I do have a melancholy about me, and all my problems are quiet ones, soft but pervasive. They tend to dull the senses, at least for a little while. Every once in a while, though, for only a day or two, I'll feel the intensity and desperation not to live. They wake me from sleep, and I'll want only to die. And maybe there is something to be said of it then. What do I have logically keeping me here, eh, Cezal? I'm rather alone—few would miss me. What kept you around, Cezal? You didn't have much to live for."

"Me? Well…" He sighed lightly. "I really don't know, I suppose. I have never felt much of a longing for death. I have been alone for most of my life, yes. Though, I am okay with it. I can't honestly say I'm happy, but again, I am okay with my dissatisfaction. I have the small things, I suppose because I just don't expect much. To look at nature and watch the sunset is perhaps a rather paltry reason to live, but for some, it brings a lot of joy. For me, it brings only some. But some is enough."

He noticed a cold cup of coffee next to him, probably from that morning, and took a sip.

"Perhaps, Alja, you should think about a higher power. For you, that could be necessary," he tried to soften his voice, "to make it easier to live."

"I haven't really thought of that." She looked straight ahead, vaguely into the distance, as though there was no wall separating her from the storm. "Wouldn't that be rather insincere?"

"No, I don't think so," Cezal said, finding more strength in his voice. "For some people, it helps them. It is a way to cope. Yes, I cannot claim that there is a higher truth to be found therein, but I don't think it's necessarily hurting you either."

"That's all you have to answer?" She looked down at him, face painted with dissatisfaction.

He issued a small yes that floundered through the dusty air. He had intended it to sound more sincere and sensitive, but it had come out wrong.

* * *

Still night. Still snow. She threw off the blankets and jumped for joy, a pure joy.

"Oh, my Cezal!" She ran over and shook him awake—spoke to him, hands on his shoulders and face, close enough to smell her breath. "This is all a dream. Can't you see? I'm not real, you're not real, nothing is. Come, let us run off together!" She began to frolic to the door and get her coat. "Emotions are the best simulator of reality. Let us leave and run away and feed off of emotion until we die in each other's minds. Come! *Come!*" She coaxed him, "Let us leave this place—there's nothing to stay for."

A cloud of realization filled Cazal. He sighed.

"I know it is snowy out," she continued, almost pleading. "We will last out there at most a couple of hours, but in that time, we will live out our entire lives with a depth and passion seldom few have experienced. We will be faced either with complete despair or complete envelopment of the other. It will be an intensity like nothing else. Don't you see Cezal?" Her eyes implored him.

He looked at her with sadness and care. "No. Come on, Alja, I think you will regret it. Let's stay here. It is nice and warm."

"No! Do not claim to know what I want! Why did I ever waste my time on you?"

"It's okay, Alja, just come back here. Yes?"

She slumped by the wood-paneled door, dejected. "Yes."

* * *

Birds flew, playing in the fresh air outside, filling the world with their spring song. The cherry trees were in full bloom. Chirp! Chirp! and then another chirp! They perched outside in between their games. Inside, the smell of jam.

"Malanta, my dear, you look sad. What's wrong?" Alja kneeled to talk with Malanta at eye level.

"At school, one of the kids in the older grades pulled my hair and made fun of how I dressed, Mommy."

"Oh, I'm very sorry to hear that, my dear." She took her hand and began to admire Malanta's little fingers—like snow peas, they were. "It may not help too much now, but people like that won't get too far. Try not to let it get to you. Think instead of your friends—surely they don't like that the older kid bullied you. And I love you very much, and you're very wanted here. And you're home now. Come, let's sit together a bit on the couch, and I'll tell you a nice story. Are you hungry? I have some raisin bread that I made earlier today."

Malanta smiled a sweet smile. "Yes, Mommy, can I have some bread?"

"Of course, my dear." And she went over to the kitchen and cut a slice of raisin bread for Malanta, with some butter and salt sprinkled on top. Then, they walked over to the couch and sat down together. Alja was resting on the sofa arm, and Malanta was leaning against her, her plate in hand with Alja's arm around her shoulder.

"Now, what kind of story shall I tell? What do you feel like hearing about today?"

"A story with a happy ending, please," Malanta asked ever so purely. And so, Alja told a nice story with an ending like warm milk and strawberry juice, and Malanta snuggled up next to her mother. Soon they both fell asleep in the light afternoon sun, Malanta's chubby little cheek squished against Alja's side.

* * *

It was daytime, and the light sprinkled itself over the land. No fog today—no, just crisp air and fresh snow.

"You know," said Alja while she and Cezal were both sitting in chairs around the table after breakfast. "There are some who say you can only truly have that which can't be taken from you."

He cocked his head. "What do you mean?"

"Well, if I stole your jacket from you and used it for myself, then could you really say it's still yours? We could agree that it's rightfully yours, but that wouldn't mean that it's not really just mine."

"Well… I suppose that's true, but what does it matter?"

"It matters," said Alja, drawing out her words and leaning in, "when you apply it to other things. Ask yourself, Cezal, by these standards, what do you actually have? What can't be taken from you? All your possessions certainly can. Your freedom certainly can. Your life, even, can be taken. What then is leftover?"

"Well…" he considered, "as I said before, we have our emotions and our experiences. Our memories…"

"And your ideas and thoughts," she added. "And that's what bothers me about the way I see people live. They take so much for granted. They don't realize how easy it is for all the things they have in life to suddenly be gone. No one is ever more than human. Sometimes it's hard to keep reminding myself that, though. *Especially* those who think

248

they deserve what they have—how I hate that word. It drips with arrogance and self-righteousness. Yes, people who think they *deserve* what they have would be well tied up by their feet to a rope and hung upside down in a river. I wonder if they would think they deserve that." She burst out laughing, intensity ringing through her eyes.

He leaned back.

"I got carried away. Don't take heed to my emotions. I speak this way only because I am bitter. My point is that those who think they deserve anything are…" She wrinkled her nose. "I don't know how to put into words my disgust for such people. But it is because they see themselves as though *above* somehow. In doing so, they spit in the face of every person who never got a chance, every person who works and gets little in return. They convince themselves they are righteous, that what they are and what they have is of their own doing, and because of that, it is rightfully theirs—that it belongs to no other. 'And why should it?' they ask. But why shouldn't it is really a far better question. They are lesser beings I have decided; less than human."

Cezal nodded tactfully. "I don't really know how to respond. I'm inclined to reject what you're saying, but if I'm honest with myself, I think you may be right to a degree, even if I don't agree with your conclusions."

Alja stared, waiting for him to say more.

"Cezal, I know *you're* at fault here." And her eyes flashed. "But I am too. All people are, or at least all people would be. The least one can do is not see themselves as moral, as though above. Everything you have, from your intelligence to your wealth, to your opinions: none of that is special, and none of that has come about through your own doing. You're sticking your head in the sand if you think anyone else born in your position wouldn't have acted in a nearly identical way. This is what I mean—people make themselves out to be too much. They think they're special when they're not. They think they're consequential when they're not. They think they will make some lasting impact when they won't. And there's nothing wrong with this, but you can always see in the way someone holds themselves. You can see it in the way they speak, the intonation of their sentences, and the subjects they choose to speak on. It all paints a picture. Most of the time it's a rather grating, ostentatious one."

Cezal sighed and looked into his bowl. It was empty. "What do you get from all this resentment for humanity, Alja? I don't completely disagree with what you say, but if you hate humanity, how can you not hate yourself? Is it worth it? What do you really gain?"

She squinted her eyes, and disgust formed on her mouth. "Because, you fuckhead, it's not good for people to exist. Really for any life to exist, but most so for humans."

"Why is that?" he asked, by this point used to her empty aggression.

"Because there's just so much pain, and how can one justify it? If there were nothing to feel pain, then it wouldn't be a problem."

"But then you wouldn't feel good things either," he countered.

"Well, yes, that follows. But does the good make up for the bad? Each exists infinitely."

"What do you mean by infinitely?" Cezal leaned forward, clasping his hands in an attempt to appear especially calm.

"Good and evil are just terms I use because it's more practical, but when it comes down to it, neither exist—they're just labels we retroactively put on events or people or whatever."

She lightly shook her head. "Really, there's suffering and the lack thereof, that's it. And there's no inherent reason for there to be any limit to that suffering or lack thereof. Therefore, they exist infinitely," she explained in lucidity.

"But don't you think that's kind of unfair to equivocate suffering to evil, and merely the lack of it to good? You don't see good as a force in itself?"

She raised an eyebrow and shook her head. "No, I don't… Though to be logically fair, it would only make sense that bad isn't a force in itself either."

"What then is there?"

"I guess then there's nothing," she said. "It's all empty."

"What's empty?"

"Everything, Cezal. Everything that we see, do, or hear is all empty. It simply *is*; that's it."

"Yes, I suppose it all is empty, isn't it," he sighed.

"Yes," she echoed, staring far away.

"But then that means we can fill it with whatever we want, does it not?" he countered, a hopeful tone tainting his voice.

"What do you mean?"

"Well, we could fill it up with the emotions we wish. You say good and evil exist infinitely, but who ultimately chooses what gets filled with what and to what extent?" Now it was Cezal's turn to raise an eyebrow. "As you've said, Alja, we're all completely alone. Who then is there but we ourselves to fill the world, to make the grass a vibrant green or a dull brown, to make the water an even deeper blue or make it evaporate entirely, to make the world shine or be shrouded by darkness?"

She nodded a bit with a dim smile. "You paint a nice picture, Cezal. I suppose we are alone, aren't we?"

"Yes. Very alone."

* * *

He came to see that with Alja, there were gray days, usually filled with thunder and lightning, and then there were blue days, with a blue sky and a warm sun. Today was a blue day. They both sat in blankets around the fire with warm water in tin cups.

"Do you remember, Cezal, when I said I see my life as a work of art, and I try to live it as beautifully as possible?"

He nodded. "Yes, I do remember that."

"I used to think of life as a book, and I was the protagonist. I think a lot of people do that, whether they realize it or not. There's something comfortable about most of the books we read. There's a rhythm they follow, and many times we already sort of know how things will end."

He smiled a bit. "Yes, I know what you mean."

"And it's nice. It's comforting. After all, why shouldn't one be the protagonist of their own life story?"

He smiled a different, more weathered smile, knowing where this was going. "It leads to disappointment, doesn't it?"

In turn, Alja gave a weathered smile of her own and looked at him. "Ah, I've become predictable, I see." And she chuckled a bit. "Yes, it leads to disappointment. It makes you believe in things that aren't there, and when you see them gone, you feel tricked and wronged. And what is one to do then?" She sighed as the flame flickered. "I think it's much better to be a painting than a book. A painting doesn't exist outside of itself, outside of that one, unique moment in time. That instant is all the painting is—that's all it ever can be. But you have it… you possess it in a way that you could never possess a story. Sometimes, I think our lives would be better if they only lasted an instant. Just one moment of love, or elation, or tenderness, or melancholy, or even dripping despair, and then death. Then our lives would truly be paintings."

Cezal sat in silence without reply, looking into the forest in the backlit midmorning sun. The sounds of the living forest, dormant in the winter, echoed through the snow and were dampened by the air.

"I hate feeling I've lived too long, Cezal. I've become bitter and senile too soon. Other people aren't like this. I don't know why I am. It's so hard not to see the futility of it all. Nothing really changes." She began to cry. "I wish it weren't like this. I wish it were different."

* * *

That night, Cezal brought out some coffee. Rye was running low. He set a cup next to Alja who had herself wrapped in a blanket.

"Do you believe in hell, Cezal?" she asked, vacantly staring into the fire.

He sat down beside her, cup in hand. "No, I can't say I do."

She nodded. "I don't either. But I think a lot about what hell would be like. Eternal burning feels rather unimaginative to me, though I can see why such a conception has been so popular. But there are many types of hell. I've been contemplating what hell would be like for me if I were its designer."

"And what would it look like for you?"

"Well, it would be my life now, but I would live knowing once I was outside of someone's line of vision, they would forget I had ever existed. I would grow up, and my parents would feed me and bathe me and do the normal things parents do, but deep in my heart, the whole time I would know the second I was out of their sight, they would forget about me and what they have done for me: everything I had ever been for them, and everything they were to me. I would only come back into existence when I reappeared again. I would know once I leave home, it would be as though I were never born. Every stranger I could have a chance encounter with would immediately forget we had ever talked. It would be as though I were a ghost. As though the entire world started and ended with other people's conception of me. I could never know anyone, and they could never know me."

"Naturally though, you would remember them, I take it?" Cezal asked, watching the flames.

"Well, of course," she said. "It only works if you're aware. I would have that pervasive sense of nobody-ness. More so than I do now. Did you know about the experiment they did on dogs? I don't remember the details, but, in short, they electrically shocked dogs. In one group, the dogs were able to turn off the shock by pushing on a lever or something like that, but in another group, there was no way for them to turn off the electrical current, and after a while, even the dogs who had been able to turn off the current before by pressing the lever realized it was no longer possible and just laid down and endured it. For that group, even after the scientists made it so that the dogs could press the lever to make the current stop, they still just lay on the ground, waiting for it to stop. Learned helplessness—that's the term."

Cezal sighed and took a sip of coffee. "I guess that's how a lot of people are… Is that what cynicism is, learned helplessness?"

They both stared into the fire, the weight of it all oppressive, but of course, not crushing.

"Maybe in a way," Alja replied, not turning her head. "I think most self-described cynics take pride in their being cynical, seeing it as a way to protect themselves from the disappointments of the world." She shrugged. "But at the same time, I suppose you find what you look for."

"Perhaps that's the difference I think between the cynics and realists," Cezal mused. "Cynicism comes from an emotional place, whereas realism comes from a pragmatic one. What may look like cynicism to some is, in fact, just pragmatism."

"Mm," Alja nodded. "But I think emotions are important. I think you yourself have spoken about their importance before."

"Oh, I agree. Between emotions and our relationships, that's really all we have, I suppose. But," he clarified, "that's not what I mean. I think many people see logic as being at odds with emotion and vice-versa, when really, I've come to see more that they work together—it's that one should be pragmatic and logical with interpreting their emotions. More often than not, they work together."

Alja nodded slowly, mulling over his words. "I see what you're saying. Perhaps you're right. But what do you think of the kind of hell I described?"

"Oh, yes, that's right," he said. "But what do you mean?"

She made no change in expression. "What if that were your world—one where no one ever remembered you. How would you handle it?"

Cezal considered it for a while, looking into the fire in the meantime. "Well, I wouldn't enjoy it, but it wouldn't be the worst thing for me. I think we all already live it, or at least some version thereof."

"How do you mean?" she asked.

"Well, ten thousand years from now, what of our time will be remembered?"

She nodded. "None of it, most likely."

"And of what is remembered, do you suppose that any of it will be so because of something we do? I think our entire lives will be lost to history," he reasoned.

Alja looked into the fire and sighed. "I know that well, Cezal. Why do you think I paint? Why do you think I try to grab the moment so frantically? I feel the anxiety of it."

She looked again into the fire, and they both were silent for some time.

"But there is a stark difference between the two, Cezal." She shook her head. "You shouldn't conflate them."

* * *

The world was cold. And the air that filled it was still, and crisp. The sun had set by then for a while and the lingering crimson of the horizon had just disappeared.

"Look at them, Cezal."

For once, the sky was clear, and they both had gone outside to watch the stars dawn.

"I see them. They're beautiful," he replied.

She laughed. "They're more than beautiful, Cezal. They are ferocious. Think of them. They are far but think of them up close. Hear their flame. Hear the explosions and the burning. The light, so bright!" Her voice was beginning to grow louder, like a kettle starting to boil. "Go there, Cezal. Be enveloped by the flame and become the star—feel the fire, feel the ferocity. The stars live, Cezal. They live as I have never lived before." She shook her head with mounting vigor. "Feel their intensity. Feel it. *Feel it.* Let it grip you and whip you about, imbue you with vigor and fervor to live, a primordial urge to live." Her hands were in fists, and she was waving them around with fire in her eyes. "Cezal, you must grab it like you would a raging bull. Get pulled and thrashed, feel yourself almost let go, focus almost solely on hanging on. Cezal, feel it. Let it tear you apart." She stopped, and for a moment, the world was filled with nothing but darkness and a pair of fiery eyes. "Do you feel it?" Silence again. "That is the will to live. That is what it means to look pure life in the face and *scream* at it, *tear* at it, and envelop it. Your soul *engorges* the star, Cezal. It swallows it. Feel the intensity. Feel the passion. You will never feel another one like it. Oh, Cezal, tonight I live. Tonight I live!" And she danced around, the dry snow getting kicked up and thrown about.

She looked at him just standing there and began again.

"Cezal! You must feel your life envelop you. Let it grab you by the throat and stuff your body with needles and *embrace* it with your whole being." She waved her arms and fists at him, shaking back and forth. "Tear them out of you and beat it to a pulp. Beat it and *become* it. Shake with fervor. *Shake*. And feel the world move to your rhythm. Cezal, it's real, it's all so very real. Do you hear it? Do you hear the call? 'The call of what?' you ask. The call of *insanity*. The call of the *ferocious*. The call of all that exists! The call of all that you will never be!" She walked toward him, vehemence pouring out of her being. "Cezal! Let it taunt you! Let it grip you! Let it fill you up and pour out of you. No one will ever love you, Cezal." And she began to dance and flail about again. "No one ever can! Embrace it, Cezal! Embrace it with your entire being, like you could with nothing else. You will see the ultimate reality of your existence Cezal. *Feel it*! You don't seem to feel it, Cezal. You aren't enveloped by it. You must embrace it, otherwise, you will never live. Cezal! *Cezal*! You must! It passes you by and the—"

She fell—a dull thud in the deep snow.

The winter air stung his nose.

She got up and faced him—looked into his being and approached again.

"You piece of shit, you will *never* be enough. No one ever is. You must look at others, and deep down, you have to hate them. Truly hate them. That is the only true respect. Feel it in your bones, let it slide between your teeth, and weave its way down your throat into your heart. Feel it. *Feel it!*" She screamed with her entire being, spittle getting on his face. The next words that were spoken were dripping with intensity and hatred. "That is what this world is, *feeling*. The craze and the fervor!" She began dancing around once again. "The ecstasy! It is all here. It is always here. I am here. I am here. No! Don't leave me," she called to him, and he turned back around. "No, I needn't have you here! Go, I hate you! But I hate you with an open heart. Don't you get it? Don't you see? The sublime, this is it. This is the sublime. Nothing is higher. Nothing is better. Be into me!" She ran to him. "Your soul must escape you and envelop the world. Eat it. Eat the world. Feel it in you. No, not your stomach. Feel it in your being. This is it. This is life. This is reality. *Eat it. Eat it. Eat it.* Scream into it. *This* is real life. *This* is what it means to live."

* * *

Water dripped from a hole in the roof, under which Cezal had placed a pail with a cloth. Now, the waterline was above the cloth. *Plink! Plink!* It woke Cezal up and his conscious began to speak to him once more. *You cannot stand the weight of doing it again, can you?*

Plink! Alja rolled over, still deep in sleep.

Normally, the voice in his head continued, *I would belittle you, but I'll be kinder this time. It is a heavy burden. So don't do it. It's not like you need to. Just leave tomorrow night—slip out, into the darkness.*

Cezal wondered what would become of Alja if he did that.

Oh I don't know, the voice replied. *But you could get help in the village—it's only an three hours away, but for some reason you don't seem to think she will get better.*

Cezal shook his head.

But of course, you can't know that.

He admitted to himself that he didn't.

Perhaps then, the voice continued, *the best course of action would be to get help once you get to civilization.*

Cezal nodded.

But do you trust her here alone?

He pursed his lips. He didn't think so, but decided not to bring her with him.

Mm. Okay then, the voice conceded, *I won't ask you why you've made that determination. I take it you'll simply inform the sheriff of the town that there's a woman in a cabin "over yonder," and she needs help?*

Cezal nodded again.

My, what reckless behavior. I suppose people really can't rely upon you to help them, can they? Okay. Do then what you think is best.

* * *

The next day was a blue day.

Alja sat at the table with her bowl of rye porridge. She didn't eat any but instead was slumped back, staring at it.

"We will always end up alone, won't we?" she asked Cezal.

"I…" he trailed off, avoiding her eyes. "I think so, Alja."

"Mm," she replied, still looking at the porridge. He began to look at it too. It didn't move.

"Sometimes," he began, "I think you just have to appreciate something for what it was. I know it's not ending the way you had hoped—but at least it was what it was, and nothing can take that away."

He kept looking at the porridge, but now she was looking up at him.

"Do you regret this, Cezal?" she asked.

"No, I don't," he replied. "We will always have the time we've shared."

* * *

The night had been cold, but Alja was wrapped up in a blanket, warm and comfortable.

Plink! The drips from the bucket woke her up into the imperceptible haze, and suddenly, she saw it was morning again. But oh, poor, dear Alja: she was alone.

"Alone? But where is Cezal?"

He must have left without me.

Tears began to flow, and the world began to crumple into itself, and she curled into a ball on her bedroll.

The world is cold. He said it himself—you will always end up alone.

She cried more. Because what else was there to do?

Eventually, she cried herself to sleep. Sometime in the afternoon, the sun reflected off of a window and was flashing in her eyes, so she woke up again. And the world dripped into her, like molasses.

Eventually, she dragged herself up and felt her joints ache. Why did she get up? There was no real reason. She stepped outside, into the snow and into the light of the sun. And to her surprise, she saw it, and it really was golden.

The world began to melt away, and along with it, all of its sundry feelings and sensations. It melted away, as though a great something had finally become a great nothing. And it was that absence—that wonderful absence that was leftover. Finally, that absence, that lack, felt perfectly real and tangible.

It's all in your head.

Well, of course it is. What else could it be? And slowly, as she looked out at the world, seeing her family, and Cezal, and Malanta, she saw she could fill it with warmth. Because she was alone. Because she would always be alone. And because it was a dream—it was all a dream. That's all it ever could be. And so, the music began to play, its melody lifting her spirits.

She took a deep breath.

Ah, it's okay. It will always be okay.

The world took on a more vibrant tone as she sat on a stool, facing the snow-covered forest.

The coming winter storms, with the coming cold and darkness: ah, so that's what it is. That's what everything is. How quaint. How comforting.

Because I will always be alone. Because I have created the world. Because it is a dream. Ah, and I love you, Cezal. I love you, Malanta. I love you, world. Because I can. And because you are nothing.

She closed her eyes and in a breath, breathed in the world. Then, she exhaled and opened her eyes, and the world was created once more, smiling and bright.

AFTERWORD

Dear readers,

Thank you for reading this book. Originally, I had not planned on writing an afterword, but as I got further and further into the editing process, I felt that it would be valuable to describe more specifically what exactly I'm trying to achieve in publishing this book. As such, this afterword is, in many ways, a further philosophical clarification on the themes and questions I addressed at the very beginning in the author's note.

I planned for the analysis of this book to function on two principal levels. The first level was simply to ask the reader what they thought about the philosophies espoused by each character. Do they agree with what Iljantva said about X subject? Has she led a good life? Was there truth to Zamen's life philosophy? Is his narrative of the modern (i.e., post-soviet) world accurate? Where does Alja's defeatism and cynicism come from? What exactly did Alja realize at the very end of the book? Was the ending optimistic or pessimistic?

* * *

The second level of analysis is intended to come out of a more contextualized understanding of each character. What kind of world surrounds each of them in order for them to view it in the way they do? What does it say about them that they view their world in this way?

While I hesitate to describe the major allegories in overly concrete terms, for fear of appearing not to leave much room for interpretation, I will describe one in relative detail.

This allegory presents each character in the book as representing a specific perspective or dynamic in our transition into the modern world, particularly the post-soviet modern world. Put in its most succinct form, Cezal represents the individual with one foot in the modern era and one foot in the time that preceded it. The train ride represents his leaving this older, more suffocating era that was dictated by tradition, social norms, and strong social ties and entering into the world of the individual. His transition culminated in his wintering in an isolated cabin with only one other person, whom he abandoned in her time of need.

Iljantva is the sage figure who is there to help Cezal and the reader have a more philosophical context to the world of *The Golden Sun* and understand how to analyze the various characters that follow her. She is representative of being a member of one of the last generations to live out the majority of their life in the time before the modern era.

Zamen represents the opportunistic forces that come into play once individuals are lost in our baseless society. While he is ostensibly an ideologue, and thus can be said to represent any politician or authority figure to some degree or another, I wrote his "nature" to function similarly to how modern technology functions. The most prominent example of this is perhaps social media, in that it openly manipulates users and actively works to change their understanding of the world, in their case to a monetary end. At the same time, the malevolent functions of social media are no secret. We know how addictive and caustic their effects are; yet, the majority of us still use and rely increasingly upon them. This is similar to Cezal, who befriends the ideologue despite knowing that Zamen sees him merely as a person to manipulate.

Lastly, Alja represents the disillusioned individual who has grown up in our modern world and who is doing their best to navigate it. Put in the most concrete of terms, she represents the spirit of all generations who have grown up after the popularization of social media and modern technology; in other words, anyone who grew up during or after circa 2010. She represents the atrophying of the human spirit that is plaguing our generation and, if nothing changes, the subsequent ones.

* * *

If there is any concrete result of this book that I hope to see, it is for the individual to do some deep and serious introspection about what they think their beliefs are and what place they think they have in the world. There is a very real disillusionment that we have at this time. We are seeing the ways in which the individual is powerless and apathetic and doesn't know what to do. We see the exploration and colonization of space as being decreasingly the subject matter of science fiction, and increasingly the material of the news; and yet, with all this fancy and shiny technology, we still see war and genocide, we see people still without food and shelter, both in the industrialized and industrializing world, and we see how each of us, as individuals, play our part in perpetuating it. It would be a false dichotomy to say you can't pursue both space exploration and the betterment of humanity, but I am writing here of an incongruence of spirit behind the two endeavors. We live in an age of foolishness, and thus we are the fools who epitomize it. For perhaps the first time in history, we are largely free of the millennia-long ideological chains that have simultaneously held us back and held us together; so now, no one knows what to do.

All of this said, it means that this book is a call-to-action of sorts. We must break out of narrow ideological views to which most people subscribe in one way or another. Perhaps the most wonderful lesson of postmodernism is that there is no greater truth or reality. As such, we must remind ourselves that the greatest treasures in all the universe are found in each other because in the end, that is all we really have. We must remind ourselves of the humanity and respect that all living beings deserve and build our societies, narratives, and ideologies around that belief. We cannot view the outside world as a resource to be exploited, but rather, we must view it, and all the beings that populate it (humans and other life alike), with deep reverence and parental desire for their well-being. That is the only way in which we can leave this tundra of alienation and disillusionment we find ourselves in.

This cannot, however, be done comfortably. Were that the case, then we would not find ourselves in the mess we currently do. It requires awareness and a desire to self-over-come. It requires humility and generosity, and the process will invariably hurt.

As Zamen himself said, we must understand that ideology and narrative are tools at our disposal—we do not inherit them any longer. Understanding this fact is a major part in cultivating the self-awareness required to overcome our lesser selves. Ideologies on their own do nothing. It is the projection of them that matters. Had Cezal grown up thinking he were a farmer, his identity and personality would indeed have been very different, but as he deftly pointed out to Iljantva, if he were to suddenly have thought he were a farmer in adulthood, it wouldn't have had any immediate effect—it is only through interacting with the world he would have started to cultivate this different understanding of himself. The same is the case for our own ideologies and narratives. We must see them as tools constantly at our disposal; tools that require respect, wisdom, and skill to use in order to cultivate a better world for all. Of course, as with all tools, we must also keep in mind that just as they adapt the world according to our desires, so too will we adapt to them. This is a foremost principle in understanding the inherent connectedness of our environment and ourselves.

We must also, as humans, remember that all these seemingly insurmountable problems that we face—all these forces that seem so unchangeable and so outside of our control—are nothing more than the manifestation of popularly held ideology. The problems of capitalism, liberalism, colonialism, democracy, and the increasing tendency toward techno-totalitarianism are all manifestations of ideology, and therefore, do not exist outside of ourselves. We cannot grow apathetic or give in to escapist tendencies but rather must cultivate our collective wisdom and rediscover our interconnectedness to overcome these ills.

In this context, how exactly we go about "rediscovering our interconnectedness" is a question of rather high importance. If we can properly answer it, we will find that the nature of many other, more ostensibly weighty problems of our times are far easier to understand and overcome.

* * *

I hope that this book not only spurs a self-reckoning among its readers but that it also provides a framework for understanding our times and thus for overcoming the problems that it will come to be epitomized by. In no way does *The Golden Sun* even come close to being comprehensive in its scope, analysis, and critique. However, what it does attempt to do is provide a narrative and starting point for further reflection and action. It is precisely the narrative that I have outlined here in this afterward that I suggest we, collectively, take up and use to our advantage.

Thank you for reading.

www.ingramcontent.com/pod-product-compliance
Lightning Source LLC
Chambersburg PA
CBHW051441050726
47593CB00005B/1875